FROM MANUSCRIPT TO MICROPHONE

The Author's Guide to Creating Audiobooks

GARY FEARON

FROM MANUSCRIPT TO MICROPHONE

The Author's Guide to Creating Audiobooks

GARY FEARON

From Manuscript to Microphone:
The Author's Guide to Creating Audiobooks

First Edition: May 2026
ISBN: 978-1-7348555-0-0

To those who have a story to tell
but haven't yet found their voice.

This is for you.

CONTENTS

PREFACE: THE SILENCE IS OVER

For centuries, the relationship between an author and a reader was a pretty quiet one. Stories were written in isolation, committed to paper, and consumed in the hush of a library or a living room chair. But in this digital age, the world of literature has found its voice.

And it is *loud.*

Today, your readers aren't just sitting in armchairs; they are commuting, exercising, and folding laundry as they listen. They aren't just looking for a story; they are looking for a voice to keep them company while they multitask. If your book only exists on the printed page, you are leaving half of your audience in the dark.

I wrote this guide because my production partner Karen Busler and I have seen too many brilliant authors stumble at the finish line. They spend years perfecting every comma, only to treat the audiobook as a technical afterthought—or worse, as an overwhelming barrier they don't feel ready to cross.

Here's the good news. You *are* ready. You wrote the book. Literally.

From Manuscript to Microphone is designed to dismantle any intimidation.

Whether you intend to step behind the microphone yourself, hire a veteran voice artist to breathe life into your characters, or explore the controversial world of AI-generated narration, our goal remains the same: to ensure that your transition from the silent page to the spoken word is seamless, professional, and profitable.

The written word may speak, but the human voice *connects*. This book embraces the philosophy that the page is a stage waiting for an actor.

The silence is over. It's time for you to be heard.

CHAPTER 1: THE INVISIBLE BOOKSHELF
WHY YOUR BOOK DOESN'T EXIST (TO HALF YOUR AUDIENCE)

You've done the hard part. You spent months—maybe years—pouring your soul onto the page. You navigated the labyrinth of editing; perhaps you've even tackled cover design and formatting. Your book is live on Amazon, and you've shared the link with the world. But there's a publishing truth most authors are completely unaware of: for a massive, rapidly growing portion of the reading public, your book is invisible.

It isn't because your cover is bad or your blurb is weak. It's because you've published something for their eyes in a world that is increasingly using its ears.

Read Between the Lines? They'd Rather Listen

The most recent publishing data confirms a shift in consumer behavior that should make every author sit up and take notice: many readers in all genres are becoming less "format flexible." Years ago, if a book wasn't available on audio, a fan may have grumbled and bought the paperback. Today, things are changing. With over 150 million Americans now identifying as regular audiobook listeners, a new trend has emerged.

When readers search for a title on their preferred platform and see only a "Print" or "Ebook" result, many don't reach for their reading glasses. They simply move on to the next title available in audio. In their minds, if they can't listen to it while they commute, cook, or exercise, the book literally doesn't speak to them.

We are living in a multitasking world; the days of sitting and reading for hours on end are a luxury many feel they can no longer afford. Readers who do find a spare hour often feel they could be doing something else at the same time. Audiobooks are the solution to modern "productivity guilt", the nagging feeling of falling behind.

Understanding Today's Reader

If you think audiobooks are a niche market that has yet to fully catch on, the 2026 landscape tells a different story. There is a fundamental shift in how we engage with information:

- **The $11 Billion Milestone:** The global audiobook market is projected to hit $11 billion this year. This isn't just growth; it's a revolution fueled by a perfect storm of technology and lifestyle changes.
- **The "Grown-Up" Boom:** The fastest-growing demographic for audio isn't teenagers—it's the 45-to-60-year-old category, which saw a 31% increase in listenership in the last year alone.

- **The Commuter Reclaim:** 62% of listeners use audiobooks to "read" during "dead time", turning their commutes, workouts, or chores into prime storytelling opportunities.

The Accessibility Revolution

Beyond convenience, audiobooks single-handly win in accessibility. For readers who have visual impairments, dyslexia, or anyone who happens to find traditional print challenging, the audio format opens the world of literature in an entirely new way. This revolution is powered by the smartphone in your pocket and the smart speakers in your home. These devices have made access to a book as simple as a few taps or a voice command.

We are also seeing the "podcast effect" in full swing. An entire generation is now accustomed to consuming spoken word content daily. This has primed listeners to seek out the long-form storytelling that only audiobooks can offer. Likewise, for those seeking a break from constant screen time, audio offers a welcome escape without the eye strain.

Professional Street Cred

In 2026, an audiobook is a badge of legitimacy. Having your title available on Audible, Spotify, Apple Books, and library apps like Hoopla tells the world you aren't a hobbyist; you are a professionally published author who meets them exactly where they are, whether that's the car, the gym, or the kitchen.

Furthermore, major audiobook platforms like Amazon allow you to post your audiobook on their site at no cost to you (asking only a percentage when it sells), offering an unprecedented opportunity to tap into a significant new revenue stream.

No one is about to suggest that print is dead. Print is wonderful! But an audiobook is the way for you to reach the "unreachable" reader. In these chapters, we'll show you exactly how to bridge that gap. Whether you decide to hire a professional to bring your characters to life or you're brave enough to step behind the microphone yourself, we're going to give you the blueprint to move your book into the ears of a whole new audience.

THE "LOST" HOURS OF THE DAY

Think about your average reader's day. Between the morning commute and the evening chores, there are anywhere from 1 to 4 hours of "ear time" available where "eye time" is impossible. If your book is only in print, you are essentially waving goodbye as they head out the door instead of joining them on their day. Audio doesn't just sell books; it buys you a place in your reader's daily routine. And routines, once formed, become habits. A listener who enjoys spending the day with you will come back tomorrow—and the day after.

CHAPTER 2: THEATER OF THE MIND

FROM WAX TO WIRELESS

Most authors view audiobooks as a modern digital convenience, like streaming music or a GPS. But the audiobook didn't start in a Silicon Valley lab; it began as a mission of mercy and a poet in a hotel.

How Did We Get Here?

The industry was born out of a profound need for accessibility. In 1932, the American Foundation for the Blind and the Library of Congress established the "Talking Book Program." These were nothing like the convenient digital files we have today; they were 12-inch vinyl records that held about 15 minutes of audio per side.

If you wanted to "read" a standard novel in 1934, you weren't carrying a phone; you were carrying a literal suitcase filled with fragile records. To listen to a book like *The Great Gatsby,* you had to physically get up and flip the record every quarter-hour. The "barrier to entry" for both the listener and the producer was massive. It required a recording studio the size of a living room and a distribution network involving the U.S. Postal Service.

For decades, audio was mainly a tool for the visually impaired or a luxury for children. It was functional, but it wasn't yet mainstream.

Theatre of the Mind: 1938 and the "Alien" Panic

As the technology improved, so did the craft of performance. By the late 1930s, radio had become the hearth of the American home, and on Halloween night in 1938, Orson Welles proved just how dangerous—and powerful—the spoken word could be.

His radio adaptation of H.G. Wells' *The War of the Worlds* was so convincingly performed as a series of "breaking news bulletins" that thousands of listeners across the country genuinely believed a Martian invasion was underway in New Jersey. People fled their homes, wrapped their heads in wet towels to ward off poison gas, and jammed phone lines in a state of total panic.

It was the ultimate proof of the "Theatre of the Mind." A single voice, backed by sound effects, could bypass the logical brain and trigger a visceral, physical response. Today, we often look back at 1938 with a smirk, thinking ourselves too sophisticated or jaded to fall for such a ruse. After all, we are surrounded by CGI, deepfakes, and 24-hour news cycles. We know when we are being told a story (hopefully)!

However, for the modern author, this sophistication creates a new challenge. Your listener's ear is highly trained. They are primed to detect insincerity. They can sense a "phoned-in" performance instantly. To reach them, you don't need to sound like a broadcast; you need to sound like a human. You don't win their trust with a trick; you win it with authenticity.

The $500 Bribe that Changed Everything

If we had to point to the moment the commercial audiobook was born, it would be January 1952. Two young college graduates, Barbara Holdridge and Marianne Roney, had a bold idea: they wanted to record the great poets of their time.

They tracked down the legendary Dylan Thomas at the Chelsea Hotel in New York. After much coaxing (and a $500 incentive), they got him behind a microphone. He read his poetry, but additional material was needed to fill the record. Taking on his best theatrical voice, the one usually reserved for the pulpit or the pub, he performed his magazine story *A Child's Christmas in Wales*. The engineer reportedly had to scramble to adjust the levels—Thomas's voice was so resonant and powerful that it threatened to blow out the VU meters!

That recording became a surprise hit. It proved for the first time that people would pay to hear a story read with professional passion. The company the women founded, Caedmon Records, became the "seed" for the entire spoken-word industry.

Holdridge and Roney were essentially the first indie producers. They took a financial risk on a single voice because they believed in the power of the performance. Today, you can set up a productive home studio for less than half of what they paid Dylan Thomas for one afternoon. The "bribe" is no longer necessary—just the courage to hit Record.

The Walkman Revolution and the Commuter Boom

In the 1970s and 80s, two things happened that paved the way for the modern author. We saw the invention of the cassette tape and the rise of the long-distance commute. Suddenly, stories were portable.

By 1987, audiobooks had officially moved out of the specialty niche; they were being sold in 75% of mainstream bookstores. A book didn't just sit on a shelf; it lived in the glovebox.

The Road Trip Exchange

Perhaps the most *driven* example of the audiobook's rise was the legendary Cracker Barrel rental program. It was the ultimate mission of mercy for the American traveler. You could pull off the interstate, rent a sprawling multi-tape western or a John Grisham thriller, and listen to it across three state lines. When you reached your destination—or just the next Cracker Barrel—you'd simply hand over your finished tapes and pick up a new adventure for the drive home.

Books were no longer tethered to a chair or a library. They were moving at 65 miles an hour. Audiobooks had become a survival mechanism for the highway, turning a sedan into a theater that went along for the ride.

Another "Martian" Miracle

If you have any doubts about why you belong in the audio market, look at Andy Weir.

In 2011, Weir was a software engineer who couldn't attract a literary agent to save his life. He decided to post his stranded astronaut novel, *The Martian*, for free on his blog. Later, at the request of fans, he put it on Kindle for 99 cents.

But it blasted off when a small company called Podium Publishing got wind of *The Martian's* potential. They negotiated audio rights with Weir even before a major print publisher (Crown) touched it. Podium paired the book with narrator R.C. Bray, whose snarky, brilliant performance turned the technical science of the book into a high-stakes thriller.

The audiobook became a massive hit on Audible *before* the book was a print bestseller. It won an Audie Award, caught the attention of major publishers leading to a multi-million dollar deal, and eventually became an Oscar-nominated film starring Matt Damon.

The Lesson? Andy Weir didn't wait for permission. He

provided the content, and the audio version was the engine that pulled his career into the stratosphere.

2026: The "Always-On" Era

Today, we've moved past the physical limitations of records, tapes, and even CDs. We have entered an age where listening is simply a part of the background of daily life. Between smartphones, smart speakers, and seamless car integrations like Apple CarPlay and Android Auto, your reader need never be more than a few taps away from your audiobook.

As we move into the next chapter, keep the "Martian Miracles" in mind. You aren't just making a recording; you are opening a door for a reader who might never have found you on a printed page.

PENCIL PUSHING

If you are over the age of 40, you likely remember the "Pencil Trick"—using a hexagon-shaped Ticonderoga to manually wind a loose cassette tape back into its housing. It was a tedious and oddly humbling ritual. Compare that to the modern miracle of today's audio. With the push of a button, total gratification is instantaneous. We have traded those plastic contraptions prone to failure for a seamless, indestructible audio stream, and your audience has never been more ready to hit "Play."

CHAPTER 3: CAN YOU HEAR YOUR BOOK?

IS YOUR MANUSCRIPT READY FOR THE MICROPHONE?

If you are a writer of fiction, it's almost unnecessary to ask that question. The simple truth is, your manuscript is ideal for an audiobook.

Whether you've penned a gritty noir or a sweeping fantasy epic, your work is already a prime candidate. Storytelling, in its most ancient and purest form, was never meant for the eye; it was born around the flicker of a campfire and an audience hanging on every word. We were listeners before we were readers.

Novels thrive in the audio format because they rely on the two things that the human voice handles best: *emotion* and *rhythm*. When a narrator breathes life into your protagonist, they aren't just reading your words; they are finishing the job you started on the page.

However, being a natural fit doesn't mean your work is entirely ready for prime time. While your plot and prose may be primo, consideration must be given to this new form of delivery. In a physical book, the reader provides the "voice" in their own head. In an audiobook, that responsibility shifts to the performer.

This means that although your story is a perfect fit, you may find that certain visual anchors—like long strings of "he said/she said" dialogue tags or complex formatting cues—need a gentle pruning to allow the performance to flow. Not to worry; we'll get into all of that later.

For now, rest assured that if you're a fiction writer, the answer to this chapter's burning question is a resounding *yes.* Your book isn't just ready for the microphone; it's been begging for it.

When Your Characters are Facts and Figures

But what if you're a writer of nonfiction or technical information? Your path to the microphone might feel a bit more obstructed. You look at your pages and see data, diagrams, or how-to instructions, and you wonder how that translates to a listener's earbuds.

Most authors assume that the audiobook has to be an exact replica of its printed counterpart. This misconception leads many authors to look at their charts, their footnotes, or their image-heavy guides and assume the door to the audio world is locked tight. They conclude that because their work is visual, it is inherently silent.

But you'll be glad to know that audiences aren't looking for a narrated Xerox of your book. They are looking for the soul of the ideas you've spent years refining. Rather than a carbon copy, some books merely need the right translation to become successful audiobooks.

The Information vs. Inspiration Ratio

To master this translation, it helps to understand a fundamental shift in how people consume the spoken word. When a reader holds your physical nonfiction book, they are in "Search" mode. They can flip to page 150, scan a table, and find a specific data point. The printed page is a high-efficiency retrieval system.

However, when that same person hits Play on your audiobook, they move into "Guided" mode. They have handed you the steering wheel. In this environment, raw information is no longer the primary goal—they want to be *inspired*.

In a nonfiction audiobook, raw data must be secondary to narrative appeal. If you read a complex spreadsheet or a long list of technical specifications, you will lose your listener. An audiobook listener can't visually skip over dense data. If the info becomes too cumbersome to follow by ear, the brain simply tunes out.

The Proof is in the Listening

So what do we do? I think you'll appreciate this success story that, on paper, shouldn't have worked.

In 2017, chef Samin Nosrat released a culinary manifesto, *Salt, Fat, Acid, Heat*. It wasn't a slim volume of weeknight meals; it was a sweeping, beautifully illustrated masterpiece featuring over one hundred recipes and nearly two hundred hand-drawn diagrams.

It won the James Beard Award, dominated the New York Times bestseller list, and spawned a hit Netflix series.

Then came the improbable suggestion to turn this visual feast into an audiobook.

A traditionalist might have pointed to the intricate illustrations and the step-by-step technical walkthroughs as evidence that an audio translation was impossible. How do you hear a diagram of a chicken being butchered? How do you listen to a list of ingredients without your eyes glazing over?

The skeptics were wrong.

Salt, Fat, Acid, Heat ended up becoming a beloved audio experience. Narrated by Nosrat herself, it earned glowing reviews from listeners who claimed it was the most informative cookbook they had ever encountered. Some didn't just listen once; they kept it on a loop.

How does a cookbook—a genre defined by visual reference—conquer a sound-only medium?

The answer is that Nosrat chose to provide the recipes as a supplemental PDF. Instead of reciting "two teaspoons of salt," she spends the audio time explaining the philosophy and stories behind the food. She focused on the foundational ideas that could be shared while the listener was driving to the grocery store, rather than the measurements they needed once they got home.

She discovered what was "listenable" and led with that. She left the more technical minutiae for the printed page or a digital supplement where it functioned best. That wasn't a compromise; it was a masterclass in adaptation.

Your Path to the Microphone

If a dense, illustration-heavy cookbook can find its way to the top of the audio charts, your manuscript can too. Whether you are weaving a fictional world or sharing technical expertise, the "voice" of your book is already there, tucked between the lines of your prose.

The question is no longer if your book should be heard. The question is: who is the right person to tell the story?

In the next few chapters, we are going to explore the three distinct paths available to the modern author. We will look at the prestige of hiring a professional narrator, the burgeoning frontier of AI voices, and the deeply personal journey

THE MALCOLM GLADWELL MINDSET

Malcolm Gladwell doesn't just record audiobooks; he creates immersive experiences. For *Revenge of the Tipping Point,* Gladwell integrated cinematic scoring and real-world interview snippets, treating the format as a primary medium rather than a secondary thought. You may not have a podcasting empire or the production budget for a full musical score, but you can borrow his mindset. Gladwell didn't ask, "How do I read my book?" He asked, "What can this book become when audio is its primary home?" Answer that question, and you stop being an author who is just "getting an audiobook done". You bring your words to life..

of stepping behind the microphone yourself.

Each path has its own set of rewards and hurdles. Let's look at them all so you can decide which one will take your book to the finish line.

CHAPTER 4: THREE PATHS TO THE MICROPHONE

FINDING THE RIGHT VOICE FOR YOUR VISION

The moment you decide to turn your manuscript into an audiobook, you are faced with a fundamental question: Who is going to be the voice in the reader's ear? This isn't just a logistical choice; it is a creative one. As an author, you have lived with these words for months or maybe even years. You know the rhythm of the sentences and the soul of the story. Now, you have to decide how to translate that soul into sound.

There are three distinct ways to bridge the gap between the page and the play button. You can voice it yourself, you can utilize AI narration, or you can hire a professional narrator. Each path has its own unique set of pros and cons. The right choice depends entirely on your goals, your budget, and your readiness to step into the "theatre of the mind."

The Solo Journey: Voicing It Yourself

There is an undeniable allure to the "DIY" route. When an author narrates their own work, it adds a layer of personal touch that a hired voice cannot replicate.

Readers often feel a deeper connection to the material when they know they are hearing it directly from the person who wrote it. So let's consider that option.

Doing It Yourself: The Pros

For many authors, your voice is an extension of your brand. If you have already built an audience through public speaking, podcasting, or video content, your readers have a pre-existing relationship with the sound of your voice. Depending on the material, hearing your thoughts through a third party could possibly feel like a disconnect. By stepping behind the microphone, you are offering an intimate, one-on-one experience that says, "I am telling this story directly to you."

Beyond the branding, there is the matter of nuance. As an author, you possess the natural instinct for your own prose. You know which words are meant to be whispered, where the sarcasm lies, or where an emotional gut-punch is hidden. You don't have to provide a "character brief" or pronunciation guide to a narrator because *you* created the characters and the world they live in. This path offers the ultimate level of creative control; you are the final decision maker of every breath and pause.

Furthermore, narrating your own work is an incredible exercise in self-editing. There is no better way to find "clunky" dialogue or repetitive phrasing than being forced to read it aloud for a microphone. Many authors discover that the process of recording their first book actually makes them a much stronger writer for book two.

If you have the equipment and the patience, this is also the most cost-effective path. You aren't paying for studio time or talent fees; you are investing your own sweat equity into a long-term asset.

Doing It Yourself: The Cons

The DIY path is paved with hidden challenges. The most significant is a lack of objectivity. Because we live with our own voices every day, we often lose the ability to hear them critically. A performance that feels comfortable in the booth might not always translate to an experienced listener's ear.

Then there's the environment. Recording an audiobook isn't just about limiting background noise; it's about achieving silence. Professional studios are soundproofed. You must eliminate the hum of a refrigerator, the distant roar of a lawnmower, or the neighbor's kid bouncing a basketball. Many authors can DIY this with egg-crate foam or heavy drapes, but achieving a broadcast-quality "noise floor" often requires technical expertise.

Finally, it will be necessary to master the computer magic of editing, mastering, and file formatting. You are essentially taking on two jobs: performer and sound engineer.

The Digital Shortcut: AI Narration

We would be remiss if we didn't discuss the "robot in the room." AI voicing has moved past the uncanny valley of synthetic stutters into a territory that is as compelling as it is controversial.

AI Narration: The Pros

The primary appeal of AI is its efficiency and affordability. For authors with a deep backlist of titles that might not justify the high upfront cost of a human narrator, AI offers a break-even point that is much easier to reach. Leading platforms like ElevenLabs have revolutionized the space with not only text-to-speech but speech-to-speech technology via high-fidelity voice cloning. This allows for a level of emotional inflection that was science fiction only a few years ago.

Additionally, AI tools are becoming increasingly adept at foreign translation. Imagine being able to offer your work in Spanish, French, or German simultaneously with the English release—without hiring a global cast of voice actors.

AI is undeniably fast and surprisingly cheap. For authors on a shoestring budget, it offers a way to enter the market without the upfront cost of a human narrator.

AI Narration: The Cons

Despite the technological leaps, AI still struggles with

interpretation. It lacks the emotional nuance required to keep a listener engaged for eight hours. An AI voice can read the words, but it cannot understand what it's reading. Audio glitches are also not uncommon, requiring tedious manual retakes and editing.

Most importantly for authors, there is a major distribution hurdle: As of this writing, many platforms have strict policies regarding AI content. While Amazon's Audible allows some use of AI (under specific "Virtual Voice" programs), they still maintain stringent gatekeeping for independent AI-generated uploads. If you want your book on the world's largest audiobook storefront, you may find that the "cheap" AI route actually ends up costing you your most important sales channel.

The Gold Standard: Hiring a Professional

If you want your book to be a performance rather than just a reading, hiring a professional narrator is the recommended path. This is the "Real Deal"—an investment in the longevity of your brand.

Hiring a Professional: The Pros

A professional narrator understands that this is not a dress rehearsal. They bring performance expertise that turns your book into an experience. Just as we go to plays or concerts to see a performance, listeners flock to audiobooks to be entertained. A pro knows how to breathe life into characters and maintain a melodic, engaging pace that keeps the listener from hitting the Stop button.

When you hire a pro, you are also hiring their studio and their producer. You don't have to worry about "noise floors" or "bit rates." You simply review the files, request any changes, and approve the final product. It frees you up to do what you do best: write your next book.

Hiring a Professional: The Cons

There is truly only one con to this path: the cost. Hiring a professional is an investment. You will face a higher upfront cost, often calculated as a "Per Finished Hour" (PFH) rate. However, much like professional cover design or editing, this is an investment that pays dividends in listener satisfaction, social media word-of-mouth, and, ultimately, higher sales. As the saying goes: *You get what you pay for.*

Because a professional narrator is the path most authors choose, we'll begin our deep dive there.

CHAPTER 5: WORKING WITH A NARRATOR

THE PRODUCTION PARTNERSHIP

Once you have decided to hire a professional, the next logical question is: Where do I find one? The search for the right voice doesn't have to be a daunting task. In fact, it should be an extension of your own love for audio. One direct route to finding a narrator is simply to listen. If you have recently enjoyed an audiobook and found yourself captivated by the narrator's delivery, there's a decent chance that they are available for hire. Most established narrators have their own websites where you can listen to samples of their work and contact them directly to solicit a quote.

The Digital Talent Hubs: ACX and Findaway Voices

While many veteran narrators maintain their own freelance connectivity, the vast majority of audio matchmaking happens on two major platforms: ACX (Audiobook Creation Exchange) and Findaway Voices (operating under the Spotify/InAudio umbrella). ACX is the Amazon-owned giant. It is basically a massive audition hall where you can post a sample of your script—say, two pages of your most challenging dialogue—and let narrators come to you. You can filter by sex, accent, and voice age, and within forty-eight hours, you'll likely have a dozen different interpretations of your characters sitting in your inbox. Findaway Voices offers a slightly more curated experience; instead of a public shout out, they often provide a Casting Director approach, presenting you with a shortlist of voices that specifically match your book's DNA.

Both platforms are free to join, and they handle the legalities—the contracts, the tax forms, and the distribution—so you don't have to be a lawyer to hire a pro. Whether you choose the massive open call of ACX or the global reach of Findaway, these clearinghouses turn a worldwide search into a weekend afternoon task.

Beyond these major platforms, you can look to your local community. Professional theater companies are a goldmine for talent. Stage actors and actresses are inherently adept at inhabiting characters and delivering dialogue with the emotional nuance your manuscript requires.

Word of mouth within the writing community is also invaluable. If a fellow author raves about their experience working with a particular narrator, be sure to get their contact information.

Successful collaborations will involve narrators who offer more than just a good voice. Teachers, for example, tend to be excellent storytellers. Public speakers are also skilled in the art of communication. When you find a narrator who treats your words with the right artistry, you've found more than a contractor—you've found a partner.

For example, Karen Busler, my go-to for female narration, has an extensive musical and broadcast background that informs her senses of cadence, rhythm, and musicality. Through Karen's ability to pivot from a street-wise detective to a bubbly child, we've tackled projects that require a high degree of emotional versatility. Having such a trusted voice on speed-dial isn't just a convenience; it's a direct route to capturing an author's vision.

The Narrator-Author Alliance

Selecting your narrator is only the first step. Once you have chosen the voice that will represent your work, you enter into a unique collaboration—a symbiotic relationship where the narrator's performance and your creative vision must become perfectly in sync. The goal is simple: to deliver your intent so accurately that the listener forgets they are hearing a recording and feels they are experiencing a story.

A well-chosen narrator is far more than just a voice; they are a reflection of you. Their primary responsibility is to inhabit the world you've built and deliver it with the appropriate pacing and emotional weight.

The Narrator as Your "First Listener"

A professional narrator is often the most attentive reader your book will ever have. Because they have to speak every single syllable, they will catch the rhythmic hitches, the accidental repetitions, and the emotional shifts that a silent reader might gloss over.

They will handle the heavy lifting—they will perform the initial read-through, mark up their own copy for emphasis, and manage the technical stamina required for multi-hour sessions.

Often working alongside a producer, the narrator will ensure that each word is captured as written. You'd be surprised how often a voice artist will unintentionally swap a word or miss a subtle inflection during a long session.

Then, before granting their stamp of approval, they follow the recording with a proofing phase—a meticulous step where the producer reviews the entire session in real time to catch any overlooked slips.

That said, you'll want to give this production partner permission to make minor variations if the audio version dictates an adjustment. For example, allow them to omit the occasional "he said" if attributions that don't seem repetitive on the printed page become insufferable when spoken every ten seconds. Trust in their ability to ensure that the final file you receive is listenable, polished, and ready for the world.

What the Author Needs to Provide

Working with a narrator is a specialized form of creative synergy. You provide the map (the manuscript), and they provide the vehicle (the voice). But for the journey to be successful, you both have to be looking at the same horizon.

When a professional narrator steps behind the mic, they are as invested in the story as you are. They aren't just reciting your words; they are interpreting your intent. In a thriller, they are calculating the tension; in a romance, they are cultivating the warmth. To get that peak performance, your job is to provide the guidance that informs their every inflection. Here's how.

Prepping Your Manuscript for the Microphone: The Pro Path

The most comforting advantage of hiring an expert narrator is that you are no longer a solo act. You have hired a specialist who understands mic technique, breath control, performing, and pacing in ways that take years to master.

That said, a narrator is not a mind reader. To ensure the final audio matches the heart of your writing, you must provide them with specific directions. This isn't about telling them how to do their job; it's about providing your clear vision so their expertise pulls in the right direction.

To get the best possible performance, provide your narrator with clear creative specifics. The more context you provide before they hit Record, the fewer corrections you'll both find yourselves having to make.

The Character Voice Guide

If your book features a wide cast of characters, a Voice Guide is essential. Think of this as a *Who's Who* for the ears. List your characters along with their age, sex and relationships to others. Equally important, note any unique speech patterns or accents. If a character is an "Eastern European rabbi" or a "little bitty girl," your narrator needs to know that before they step into the booth.

This doesn't need to be a hundred-page document, but a voice guide should cover the essentials:

- **The Basics:** Age, sex, and core personality.
- **The Nuance:** Is the character a fast talker? Do they have a hesitant, gravelly, or melodic voice?
- **The "Vibe":** Does the protagonist sound like a meek small-town librarian or an earnest high-school teacher?

Don't bother with physical descriptions. A narrator doesn't need to know a character is six feet tall; they need to know if that character speaks with the weary weight of a man who hasn't slept in three days.

Avoid: "John is a bartender with a ZZ Top beard."

Use: "John is cynical and worldly-wise. Think of a veteran bartender who has heard every hard-luck story in the city but still keeps the light on for his regulars."

The Pronunciation Key

Nothing pulls a listener out of a story faster than a mispronounced name or technical term. If your manuscript includes "world-building" names, unusual surnames (for example, *Toussaint*), or specialized lingo, include a phonetic guide or even record a snippet to let them hear how you say it. Your narrator may have had high school French or possess a knack for accents, but they shouldn't have to guess your intent.

Give your narrator a simple table of:

Proper Names: Especially if they have unique spellings.

Technical Terms: Industry-specific jargon.

Fictional Places: If you made it up; you decide how it's said.

Genre and Tone

The "sound" of your book is dictated by its genre. A high-stakes thriller requires urgent, tight pacing, while a warm romance needs a softer, more melodic approach. Nonfiction, on the other hand, requires a tone that is either authoritative or friendly, depending on the subject. Before recording begins, discuss the vibe of the book. Do you want the narrator to sound like a trusted mentor, a snarky coworker, or a mysterious stranger?

THE CARLIONI LESSON

Sometimes even a veteran narrator needs a creative nudge. That's when the narrator-producer alliance comes in handy. One of Karen's audiobook projects featured Detective Carlioni, a gritty cop from Brooklyn. As a native southerner, that specific New York state of mind didn't come naturally. Drawing on my Boston roots, I gave her a practical tip: "Drop the 'R' sounds. Add a little swagger." We leaned into the accent together until Carlioni walked into the room. Karen got so deep into the role that she stayed in that Brooklyn headspace for hours after the session ended! That's commitment. And the value of a production partnership.

The Tonal Roadmap

A book is a journey, and the narrator needs to know where the peaks and valleys are. Provide a brief "cheat sheet" of the book's emotional arc. If Chapter 7 is a quiet, somber reflection and Chapter 8 is a high-octane chase, tell them. This allows the narrator to "gear up" and manage their vocal energy so the performance doesn't sound flat.

The Approval Process: A Stress-Free Feedback Loop

This is a remote collaboration. You don't need to be in the studio (and, frankly, most narrators prefer the solitude of the booth and perform better when they can focus on the performance). Communication happens via email or phone, allowing you to review files at your own pace while you continue your daily life.

One of the greatest fears authors have is the "10-hour disaster"—receiving a finished audiobook only to realize they hate the tone used for the protagonist. Not to worry! Professionals use a structured approval process.

The Feedback Loop (The First 15 Minutes)

Standard industry practice is for the narrator to send you the first 15 minutes of your project. This sample will be emailed to you for approval. Listen to this carefully for such things as:

Pacing: Is it too fast or two slow?

Character Accuracy: Does "Joseph" sound like the Joseph in your head?

Tone: Is the "soul" of the book coming through?

If a character's voice isn't quite right, don't hesitate to say so. A true professional narrator doesn't place a limit on retakes; their goal is a satisfied customer and a project they are also proud to put their name on.

Note: Once you approve the First 15, the narrator will use that as the template for the rest of the book. Speak up now, or forever hold your peace!

As each audio file comes in, listen for accuracy and energy. Does the narrator's approach shift when the scene gets tense? Are the character voices distinct enough that the listener knows who is speaking without needing "he said/she said" tags?

When you provide feedback, be specific. Instead of saying "Make it better," try "Can we make this scene feel a bit more urgent?" or "This character sounds a bit too friendly here—remember, he's worried about his bar exam."

By the time the final credits are recorded, you won't just have digital files ready for uploading. You'll have a performance that breathes a second life into your written words. You've hired an expert to handle the heavy lifting so that you can stay in the headspace of your next book.

The "Math" of a Masterpiece

And now, here's what you've probably been on the edge of your seat waiting to find out. The fair question authors ask is: "How much is a narrator going to cost?"

While every project is unique, the industry standard is usually calculated "Per Finished Hour" (PFH). Simply put, you can expect to pay anywhere from $100 to $400 per finished hour for a high-quality professional. If you are seeking a celebrity voice, that rate can easily climb to $1,000 or more.

It's important to understand exactly what you are paying for. A single finished hour of audio represents as much as eight hours of labor. This includes the prep work, the actual recording, the editing to remove breaths and clicks, the "mastering" to meet platform standards, and the final quality control. A six-hour audiobook is essentially a full workweek for the production team. Realistically, the process will be spaced out over weeks (versus a recording marathon), giving both the narrator and the author breathing room between sessions.

Most professionals operate on a 50/50 payment model: half at the start of the project and the remaining half once the final files are approved and ready for upload. This protects both parties and ensures the project stays on schedule.

Authors often cite what their own time is worth as a determining factor. If it takes roughly forty hours of labor to produce a six-hour audiobook, those are forty hours you don't spend writing your next manuscript. For the career-minded author, the math is simple: by outsourcing the production, you aren't just buying a voice; you are buying back your creative life.

You will find people online offering to narrate your book for $50 or even as low as $25 PFH. Buyer beware! At that price, they aren't editing, they aren't mastering, and they likely aren't using professional equipment. A cheap audiobook that sounds like it was recorded in a bathroom will get 1-star reviews that can haunt your book's reputation forever.

The "Buy Once" or "Pay Forever" Dilemma

When using platforms like ACX, you'll encounter

an option called "Royalty Share". On the surface, it's tempting: you pay the narrator $0 upfront, and let them take 50% of your royalties for seven years.

Bottom line: If you believe in your book's long-term success, pay the PFH (Per Finished Hour) rate upfront. It's a larger pill to swallow today, but you retain 100% of your earnings for the life of the book. Use Royalty Share only if you are on a shoestring budget and your narrator is as invested in the gamble as you are.

Trust in the Power of Pro Audio

The Audio Publishers Association (APA) reports that nearly 75% of the most successful independent titles are voiced by seasoned professionals. This isn't because authors can't read their own work; it's because the modern listener's ear has become meticulously tuned to high quality audio.

In this industry, your "voice" is your "brand." It's worth doing right. Hiring a professional is the most direct route to a polished, "radio-ready" product that allows you to step back, put on your headphones, and finally experience your own story as a listener.

CHAPTER 6: AI NARRATION

THE THREE E'S: ELEVENLABS, ETHICS, AND THE ENSEMBLE CAST

Well, it's time to tell Siri to step aside. The voice in your phone has graduated from reading the weather to reading the room. Synthesized speech is getting eerily proficient. AI voices no longer sound like you're on hold; they breathe, they pause, they can even mimic international accents without needing a dialect coach.

If you are an author working on a small budget, the appeal is obvious. AI is low cost, instantaneous, and allows you to hit Publish on an audio version on the same day with your eBook. For a 300-page corporate compliance manual, AI is a logical choice. It delivers information with cold, calculated clarity. But as we move from "information" to "imagination," the silicon voice begins to show its seams.

Entering the Uncanny Valley

The primary catch with even the most advanced AI is a fundamental one: The robot doesn't know what it's saying. It is a statistical engine, not a storyteller.

A professional narrator understands that a specific line of dialogue on page 200 is a sarcastic callback to a joke from Chapter Three. They know to slow their breathing during a moment of grief or to sharpen their tone during a confrontation. By contrast, AI treats every sentence with equal competence. It interprets punctuation, but it cannot interpret subtext.

Everywhere we turn, we are increasingly experiencing the so-called Uncanny Valley of audio. That's the point where a voice sounds almost human, but something subtle—a lack of true emotional credibility—triggers a rejection response in the listener's brain. For fiction, memoirs, or inspirational nonfiction, this emotional flatlining can be a dealbreaker.

The ElevenLabs Phenomenon

If you've done any research into AI narration, you've likely encountered ElevenLabs. As of 2026, they have effectively set the standard for what text-to-speech can do. Their library of available voices is staggering—ranging from gruff, grandfatherly tones to bright, energetic marketing voices.

What makes ElevenLabs different from the robotic voices of the past is their Contextual Awareness. Their algorithms don't just read words; they scan the surrounding sentences to attempt the appropriate emotion. If a sentence ends with an exclamation point, the AI knows enough to lift the energy. If the text describes a quiet, late-night conversation, the AI can curb its enthusiasm to match that mood.

The Cast in the Machine

A dramatic development in recent months isn't just that the voices sound better; it's that they're multiplying. Traditionally, an audiobook was a solo performance. One narrator did all the work. If you wanted a full cast production, you needed a Hollywood budget.

Today, AI platforms like ElevenLabs have effectively enabled the ensemble cast. With a single subscription, an author can assign a different digital voice to every character in their book. You can have an Alabama judge, a high-pitched witness, and a neutral narrator all interacting in the same scene. You can even give a character the cloned voice of John Wayne or Michael Caine, if you're willing to pay a very high premium.

The Cautionary Note:

While a full cast sounds appealing on paper, it introduces the risk of inconsistency. An audiobook benefits from a unifying soul. If your protagonist sounds like a Shakespearean actor but your antagonist sounds like a late-night radio DJ, the common thread of the story is broken. Sonic considerations such as audio compression and equalization also tend to vary from

AI voice to AI voice. A single professional human narrator provides a consistent vocal anchor and emotional arc that ties the entire world together.

ElevenLabs is working on multi-speaker synthesis, but for now, each voice has to be recorded separately and stitched together in post-production.

> **AI ETHICS CHECK**
>
> **Consent:** Did you use a voice you have the explicit, documented right to use? If it's a "Pro Voice" from a library like ElevenLabs, ensure your subscription tier covers commercial distribution.
>
> **No "Deepfakes":** Does the voice sound suspiciously like a famous actor or a recognizable narrator? Platforms now use biometric fingerprinting to block "unauthorized likenesses."
>
> **The Metadata Mandate:** Most major platforms now require an "AI-Narrated" or "Synthesized Voice" tag in the metadata. Attempting to "hide" AI narration can lead to a permanent ban from Audible.

Ethics: The "Digital You" and Voice Passports

As an author in 2026, you must navigate a new ethical minefield. An appealing option today is cloning your own voice. You record a few sample sentences, and the AI "learns" your unique timbre. You then upload your manuscript, and tell "Digital You" to read the book.

Cloning yourself is totally ethical. It is your intellectual property, and it allows you to maintain your "brand voice" without spending sixty hours in a booth. The results you get during a given session will vary from a remarkable replica of your voice to a not entirely convincing caricature.

It is strictly forbidden (and just plain illegal) to clone another human voice without their permission or an explicit license. If you love a narrator's voice, you cannot simply feed their voice into an AI to grace your book for free. As of this writing, Spotify and Audible utilize detection tools—digital IDs—to determine whether you have the legal right to the voice you are using. If you can't prove consent and commercial licensing through these credentials, your book will be flagged and removed.

The *Charlotte's Web* Test

At our live presentations, we often conduct a simple experiment. We play a clip of a top-tier AI reading a passage from a classic like *Charlotte's Web*, followed by a live reading by Karen.

The AI is technically perfect. It hits every comma and pauses at every period. It sounds "pleasant." But it fails the Intent Test. When the character says, "You're terrific as far as I'm concerned," replied Charlotte sweetly, "and that's what counts. You're my best friend and I think you're sensational", the AI expresses all the affection of a news anchor.

When Karen reads that same passage, you can hear the smile in her voice—the kind that only comes from one friend looking another in the eye. She understands the impact of a scene that has touched many a heart. AI is excellent at delivering information, but humanity requires a human.

In a world increasingly saturated with fakery and synthetic content, a living voice is a literal breath of fresh air.

The 2026 Verdict: When to Go the Robot Route

If you're using AI legitimately and are willing to disclose the use of computer generated voices when uploading to Audible (and you *will* be asked), then the above regulations needn't deter you.

The Case for AI: Use it for purely functional nonfiction, technical manuals, or "feeder" content like short blog posts and YouTube scripts. It is a formidable tool for getting vital information directly to the listener.

The Case for Human: If you want to move a reader to tears, keep them on the edge of their seat, or build a deep, personal connection with your audience, you still need a heartbeat behind the microphone.

The "Audio Tag" Toolkit

If you've decided that AI narration is the route to take for your book, you'll get the best results by prompting your chosen AI generator with specific "Audio Tags". This gets a little technical, but you're a writer—you already know how to use symbols and syntax. Now, you're just doing it to direct a digital performer.

Here's a short list of the essential tags to help you communicate with your synthetic spokesperson. Think of these tags as "Director's Notes" that the AI reads but the listener never hears. In 2026, the ElevenLabs v3 model allows you to drop these directly into your text within [brackets] to shift the performance in real-time.

Emotional Anchors: You can steer the "soul" of a sentence by lead-in tags like [whispering], [shouting], [sobbing], or [dying of laughter].

Biological Realism: To break that Uncanny Valley feel, try inserting non-verbal cues. A well-placed [sigh], [sniff], or [soft chuckle] can make a digital voice feel suddenly, surprisingly human.

Pacing Cues: If the robot is rushing, use [pause] or [hesitates]. If a character is panicked, use [rushed] or [overlapping] to simulate that breathless energy.

Because the robot doesn't have a soul, it's your job to simulate one using these audio tags and additional punctuation. You aren't just uploading text-to-speech dialogue; you are programming a performance.

While a human narrator will see an exclamation point and know to add a touch of "awe," the AI might just get louder. By adding [awe] or [hushed excitement] before that sentence, you are giving the machine subtext.

Prepping Your Manuscript for the Microphone: The AI Path

Before you hit Generate, use this checklist to ensure your manuscript is machine-ready:

1. Punctuation Hacks

AI interprets punctuation as physical instructions. To get a human rhythm, you must sometimes over-punctuate your text:

The Ellipsis (...) : Use this for a soft, thoughtful pause. It tells the AI to hold its breath without dropping the pitch of the sentence.

The Em-Dash (—) : Use this for a sudden pivot or an interruption. It creates a "staccato" energy that feels much more natural in dialogue than a comma.

Double Paragraph Breaks: If you need a significant "beat" between ideas, hit Enter twice. The AI will translate the white space into silence.

2. Audio Tags (Those Director's Brackets):

With the ElevenLabs v3 model, bracketed instructions like these tell the AI how to feel.

Emotions: Use [excited], [whispering], [sad], or [shouting] before a line of dialogue.

Humanisms: Fabricating some flesh and blood by inserting [laughs], [sighs], or [clears throat] can add a layer of biological realism.

The "Reset": If the AI gets too "carried away" with an emotion, use [neutral] to bring the voice back to a steady baseline.

3. Master the Sliders (The Dashboard)

Don't leave ElevenLabs voice settings on "Default." You want to tune the engine for your specific genre:

Stability: For Nonfiction: Set this High (60%–80%) for a consistent, authoritative "news anchor" delivery. For Fiction: Set this Low (30%–45%), allowing for more dramatic swings in pitch and emotion.

Style Exaggeration: Keep this at 0% for most projects. Turning this up can make the AI sound unstable or "theatrical" in a way that feels fake. Use it only for extreme character voices (like a cartoon villain).

Similarity Boost: If you are cloning your own voice, keep this around 75%. Too high, and you'll start to hear digital artifacts (static or buzzing).

.

4. The Phonetic Override

The AI will eventually find a word it cannot pronounce (especially in sci-fi or technical manuals). When this happens, stop fighting the spelling and write for the ear.

If it stumbles on "niche", write it as *neesh*.

If a name like Siobhan confuses it, write *Shiv-on*.

Pro-Tip: If the AI is clipping the end of a word, try adding a random consonant or a period at the end to force it to finish the sound.

5. The "Block" Workflow

Never render an entire chapter at once. AI "drifts"—the longer it speaks, the more likely the voice is to change pitch or speed. Break your chapters into small blocks of no more than 2,000 words at a time.

The Lead-In: When recording each new block, include the last sentence of the previous block. This will prime the AI's memory so the tone remains consistent between files. You can simply snip the duplicate sentence out when you edit the sections together.

To AI or Not to AI?

Ultimately, the choice between silicon and soul isn't about right or wrong. It's about the intent of your project. If you are a nonfiction author looking to rush out your information, a technician creating a manual, or a writer with a massive backlist that would otherwise never see the light of audio, AI can be a strong ally. It widens the net, finally giving a voice to the 70% of titles currently trapped in silence.

As for the Great American Novel, the heart-to-heart memoir, or the story that relies on the subtle crack in a character's voice during a moment of grief? The human ear still knows the difference between a calculated pause and a genuine breath. In an era where fakery is becoming the default, a human voice is no longer just a choice—it is a premium brand asset.

Whichever you choose, whether it's the efficiency of AI generated voices or the artistry of a narrator, the most important step is simply this: *Choose to be heard.* In the next chapter, we'll jump into your most hands-on option for creating audiobooks.

CHAPTER 7: THE DIY DECISION

THE BRAVE NEW WORLD OF THE AUTHOR-NARRATOR

If you have read the previous chapters and decided that your voice is the only one that can truly tell your story, welcome to the frontier. You are joining a growing legion of author-narrators who are taking full control of their creative output. But before we talk about microphones or software, we need to address the most common hurdle every DIY narrator faces: The sound of your own voice.

It is a universal truth that almost nobody likes the way they sound on a recording. When we speak, we hear ourselves through a flattering combination of bone and air conduction. Our skulls, bless them, are quietly conspiring to make us sound better to ourselves than we do to anyone else. The microphone, unfortunately, is not in on the conspiracy.

The Harmonica in the Room

I learned this lesson the hard way when I was sixteen. My parents had given me my first tape recorder, and I spent hours playing DJ—introducing records and making up comedy skits with my cousins. I felt invincible behind that plastic microphone as I emulated my entertainment heroes of the day.

Then came a fateful party. To capture some "real audio" I placed a microphone in a friend's living room to record the festivities. When I pressed Play the next day, I barely recognized the person talking. My candid voice was monotone, with a thin, reedy quality as unsophisticated as a harmonica. It was an unpleasant awakening, but it was also a turning point. I didn't like what I heard, so I pledged to change it.

I went to the library, borrowed a book on how to improve a voice, and began a journey toward what was to become a lengthy career in broadcasting.

The Casey Kasem Secret

If you are paralyzed by the quality of your voice, find comfort in this advice from the legendary Casey Kasem. As the host of the weekly countdown show *American Top 40*, Kasem was one of the most recognizable voices in radio history. Yet, he famously professed, "I have a terrible voice, but I know how to communicate." His secret was *relatability.* He didn't focus on being a "voice god"; he focused on being a friend to the listener.

If you can communicate your passion for your subject, your voice quality becomes secondary. An audience will forgive a voice that isn't radio-perfect.

The DIY Litmus Test

If you are considering narrating your own book, you'll do well to conduct your own "Living Room Party" experiment.

Record 15 Minutes. Don't read a script you've rehearsed. Read a mid-book chapter that has both dialogue and description. You can just use your phone—the quality doesn't matter yet; the *performance* does.

Now, the "cringe" check: Listen back. Do you sound like you're reading to a classroom of first-graders, or are you telling a story to a friend?

The Authenticity Edge

Lest you think I'm trying to scare you off, allow me to share some encouragement. In my writers' group, I wanted to produce an audiobook of short stories written by our members. Rather than use one narrator, I invited each writer to perform his or her *own* story. One by one we worked out schedules for them to come to my studio.

As you can imagine, they were a little nervous. (And as the producer, so was I!) These weren't performers; they were writers. But as we recorded each story, I was floored. Since they had written the words, they knew exactly where the emphasis belonged. They knew the soul behind every sentence. Their *authenticity* made up for their lack of professional training.

If your book is a memoir, a personal manifesto, or a

deeply felt piece of fiction, your "non-professional" voice might actually be its greatest strength.

How Much "You" Should Be in the Booth?

Newcomers are often caught in a tug-of-war over which vocal approach to use. *Should I put on a "radio voice"? How much of my own personality should I be putting into this?* The good news is that the decision has already been made for you by the author (you)! The text itself will be your guide.

Generally, third-person narration falls into three categories, and identifying yours will tell you exactly how to read:

The Objective Observer: This is a distant, impartial narrator. Think of historical fiction or sweeping epics. You are simply reporting what is happening from a high vantage point. Your voice should be steady, unemotional, and authoritative.

Tuned In to the Action: This narrator is closer to the characters and invested in the point of view. You maintain a steady delivery but your volume and pacing can reflect the rise and fall of the action.

In the Trenches: This narrator is right there with the character, mirroring their emotions. If the character is terrified, your pacing should reflect it. If they are in love, your tone should soften. You are allowing yourself to feel what the character feels.

As for voicing the characters themselves, that's a science unto itself, and we'll get into all that in Chapter 8.

ONE SENTENCE, SIX STORIES

Karen often uses a simple six-word sentence to demonstrate the power of inflection: "I never said you stole money."

Depending on which word you emphasize, that single sentence can have six different meanings. If you emphasize "I," you're suggesting someone else said it. If you emphasize "money," you may be suggesting they stole something else, and so forth.

DIY means you don't have to coach or provide an emotion guide to a narrator since you possess the author's ear—the ability to hear the feeling and subtext exactly as it was meant to be delivered.

Selectively Passionate

We talked about Casey Kasem's "terrible" voice earlier. His secret wasn't just about coming across as a friend; it was about passion. When you care about what you are delivering, your voice naturally becomes amped up.

When narrating, pick certain words to emphasize. When we talk normally, we don't give every word the same weight. Learn to "throw away" the small words—the the's, and's, and of's—by saying them slightly faster and softer. This allows the contrast of your more important words to stand out like mountain peaks. Dismissing the lesser verbiage isn't "lazy" speech; it's strategic emphasis.

Speaking of the word "the", amateur narrators have a tendency to pronounce it "thee" no matter what word follows it. That's okay for "thee apple" but not for "thee banana". Use the long "thee" only when the next word starts with a vowel (*thee* apple, *thee* orange); otherwise, stick to the soft "thuh".

Similarly, for the article "a", there are almost *no* occasions when you should use the long "ay" sound. Go with *uh* exclusively.

Beyond the Voicing Itself: Are You Up for It?

Before you press the red Record button, you must perform a psychological and physical audit. While the cost savings are significant, DIY narration is nowhere near "free." You are paying with your most valuable currency: time.

The Stamina Test

Narration is a physical endurance sport. Can you speak clearly, with consistent energy, for ninety minutes at a stretch? By the third hour, your voice may get croaky, your stomach may start growling (which a professional mic will pick up), and your focus will begin to waver.

If you find yourself getting bored while reading your own book, you can be sure your listener will be twice as bored. To keep them engaged, *you* must be engaged.

Treat the microphone like a single person sitting across from you in your living room. You aren't "announcing" your book to a crowd; you are confiding with a friend.

We also recommend keeping a professional throat spray such as Clear Voice handy for those moments when your voice starts to tire out.

The Objectivity Factor

Can you hear your own mistakes? When we read our own work, our brains often "auto-correct" typos or missed words. A DIY narrator must be hyper-vigilant, ensuring that every "the," "and," and "but" is captured exactly as it appears in the manuscript. You might find yourself involuntarily rewriting or editing a passage as you narrate. (Which is technically okay as long as you're the author!)

One practical remedy is to follow along with your finger or a pen as you read, physically anchoring your eye to each word rather than letting your brain race ahead and fill in what it expects to find. It sounds almost comically simple, and yet professional narrators swear by it. Your brain is an enthusiastic editor who has read this manuscript fourteen times and has opinions. Your finger is a more reliable witness.

It also helps to listen back to each session before you step back into the booth. On playback, you will catch things that sailed past you in the moment. Develop the playback habit early, and it will save you considerable re-recording time later.

And on the subject of listening back, brace yourself. Like I said at the beginning of this chapter, the first time you hear your recorded voice in full flow, your brain is going to stage a minor protest. The voice in your headphones is almost always a shock, and almost nobody falls in love with it on the first date. But give it two or three sessions before you file for divorce.

What initially sounds odd almost always begins to sound natural—and likely quite good—once your ear has had time to adjust to the reality of how you actually sound rather than the flattering James Earl Jones version your skull has been playing you all these years.

Now that you feel comfortable in your narrator's skin, something wonderfully complicated is waiting for you just around the corner. Because a narrator, however assured, is only half the population of your book.

The other half is noisier, less predictable, and—if we're being honest—considerably more fun.

It's time to meet your characters.

CHAPTER 8: GETTING INTO CHARACTER

VOICING YOUR ENSEMBLE CAST

You're not an actor. Let's start there, because it's the most liberating thing you'll hear in this chapter. You aren't auditioning for a role, and you aren't expected to summon the ghost of Meryl Streep. You do not need to make your sixty-year-old Southern sheriff sound authentically different from your Bronx street kid, your British aristocrat grandmother, nor the talking cat who saunters into somebody's dream.

The only thing you truly need to do is make sure your listener knows who is speaking, and make them believe, even for a heartbeat, that the character speaking is real.

The Author's Advantage

You know every one of these people. You built them from the marrow up. You know exactly what your sheriff means when he says "fine" in a particular, clipped way—and you know it doesn't mean *fine* at all. You know which of your characters swallows her real feelings and which one wears his on his sleeve. You know the subtext, the history, and the wound beneath the words.

A professional narrator has to work hard to find those things. You? You already have them. Your job isn't to perform them; it's simply to let them out.

The goal of DIY character work isn't "theatre"—it's *differentiation* and *consistency*. Consider these your factory settings for every scene you record.

Differentiation: Can the listener tell that the Narrator has stopped talking and a Character has started?

Consistency: Does that character sound the same at hour twelve as they did at hour one?

If you can achieve those two things, you have done your job and done it well. You don't need to be a vocal chameleon. Check these two boxes and the 'theatre' will take care of itself.

The Casting Couch: Finding the Voice in the Verse

Before the microphone is plugged in and the Record button is pressed, you need to spend some quality time with your characters. I'm not talking about your mental image of them; I'm talking about their actual, physical, audible voices.

Professional voice artists often use a technique called Linear Reading: they pull every line of a single character's dialogue and read it aloud, in one sitting, start to finish. Don't skim. Don't "hear" it in your head. Actually speak the lines.

You'll be surprised at what this approach reveals. You will discover rhythms you didn't consciously write—pauses that appear naturally, a tendency toward stilted sentences, or a melodic energy that belongs to them and no one else. As you rotate through your cast, ask yourself these four "DNA Questions" for every significant character:

What is their Tempo? The person who measures every word like a diamond merchant is a different human being from the one who tumbles over their sentences in a rush to be understood.

How is their Enunciation? Are they precise and crisp with their consonants, or do they swallow their words? A character who mumbles their way through a sentence tells us everything we need to know about how they move through the world.

What is their Undercurrent? This is the "secret sauce." What emotion lives innately just underneath their words, even when they're saying something neutral? Is Marcus permanently slightly amused? Is Sarah perpetually on the verge of losing her patience? Finding that undercurrent is the difference between a voice and a performance.

The Voice Bible

Once you've found the "vibe," lock it down. A simple Voice Bible is worth its weight in retakes.

Marcus: Slow, low, never quite finishes his sentences, permanently slightly amused.

Sarah: Precise enunciation, upper midrange, prone to exasperated breaths.

One sentence is enough to orient you at the start of every session. It saves you from the creeping horror of listening back to Chapter Fourteen and realizing Marcus has mysteriously transformed into someone else since Chapter Three.

The DIY Trio: Pitch, Pace, and the Accent Trap

Every vocal distinction you create comes down to three primary tools: Pitch, Pace, and Accent. They are not created equal. Understanding their relative power—and their relative pitfalls—will save you a world of anguish at the mixing board.

1. Pitch: The Reliable Foundation

Pitch is the most dependable tool. Even a modest shift up or down from your natural register signals to a listener that someone new has entered the room.

The key here is subtlety. If you go too dramatic, you'll end up in Saturday morning cartoon territory. Think of it less as "doing a voice" and more as finding a slightly different "home base" for each character.

For example:

The World-Weary Detective: Drop the voice a few notes into the chest.

The Nervous Intern: Lift the voice a few notes higher, around your eyes and nose.

Most importantly, pitch must be sustainable. A voice that sounds great for three minutes might be physically impossible to maintain for a three-hour session. A growling prison guard may get the point across, but if it hurts your throat, it's not a character; it's a liability.

2. Pace: The Secret Weapon

Pace is often the most natural tool for an author to deploy because it requires zero physical strain. It's simply a change in how you inhabit time.

The Deliberate Thinker: They measure their words. Let the silence between sentences do the work.

The High-Velocity Talker: They are barely keeping up with their own brain. Let the words collide.

Varying the pace gives the listener's ear a completely different experience of each character without you having to change a single thing about your vocal cords.

3. Accent: The Siren Call

The accent is the tool you will most want to use, but the one you need to approach with the highest level of caution. It's seductive because it feels like the fastest route to a vivid character. However, it's treacherous because it is the hardest to sustain.

The Pro Secret: Capture the music, not the phonetics. Every accent has a "lilt"—a relationship with rhythm and emphasis.

The Irish Lilt: A melodic rise and fall.

The Southern Drawl: An unhurried ease, as if the words have all afternoon to get where they're going.

Having spent years in both New England and the southern U.S., I can pull off a Boston accent or a Tennessee twang with lived authenticity that would make them effortless to sustain for an entire book. On the other hand, I can do a credible Ronald Reagan or Sean Connery impersonation using the single words "Well" or "Yes", but maintaining either for hours like my friend Paul Shanklin—the man of a thousand voices for national radio—could do, is a feat few can boast.

Ask yourself honestly: Can I keep this accent going consistently for the full length of this book, across multiple recording sessions, including the sessions when I am tired and slightly under the weather and I'm out of coffee? If the answer isn't a stone cold *yes*, then imply the accent rather than perform it.

Vocal Shape-Shifting: Voicing Beyond Your Own Skin

Two questions generate more author-narrator anxiety than almost any other: How do I voice a character of a different sex? and How do I voice someone significantly older or younger than myself? The answer to both is the same, and it is profoundly reassuring: You are not trying to impersonate. You are trying to *suggest*.

Getting Sexy

A male author voicing a female character doesn't need to "falsetto" his way through her dialogue. A female author voicing a male character doesn't need to drop into an unconvincing, gravelly rumble. That often pulls the listener out of the story and into parody.

Instead, find what is specifically true about this particular person. Don't aim for "a woman's voice" as a category; aim for this woman's history, her specific wit, her unique impatience. Moving the voice higher or lower in your own comfortable range is enough to orient the listener. If you get her rhythm and emotional landscape right, the listener's brain will fill in the rest.

The Weight of Years (Age)

Age operates on the same principle. An elderly character isn't just a "creaky voice" and a slow trail-off—unless that is specifically who that person is.

What age actually bestows upon a character is a different relationship with time and urgency. An older character might have a different weight to their words or a hard-earned lack of irony. Let that perspective inform the voice rather than reaching for the theatrical shorthand of an "old person voice." Your listener will find it far more convincing, and your vocal cords will find it far more sustainable.

The Child Warning

Children's voices deserve a specific warning: If your natural register doesn't lend itself to going high, resist the urge. A high-pitched child voice, lasting more than a few sentences, tips quickly from cute to grating. Instead of manipulating pitch, focus on energy. Children often speak with a sense of immediate urgency; everything is new, everything is happening now, and nothing is filtered through adult world-weariness. A slightly faster pace and a brighter, more "forward" energy will signal childhood far more effectively than a squeak would.

A Cast of Thousands: Managing the Crowd

Here is a piece of advice that runs counter to every instinct you have as a novelist: Not every character needs a distinct voice.

Walk-on characters—the waitress who delivers one line of dialogue, the police officer in the crowd, the nameless colleague who says "good morning"—do not need a carefully constructed vocal identity.

Giving a bit player a distinct accent or pitch is a fast track to exhausting your listener and burning through your vocal range before your protagonists even get in the room. Your regular "Narrator's Voice" is generally adequate for the background cast. Save your vocal cords for the characters who have earned it.

The Battle Against Vocal Drift

For your primary cast—the ones who carry the emotional weight of the story—consistency is your greatest challenge. Vocal drift is real, it is gradual, and it is merciless. It can drift most dramatically between Tuesday's session and Friday's session.

If a character's voice shifts subtly over ten chapters, your listener's subconscious will register it as a nagging sense of unease—a feeling that something is off without knowing why. Consistency is the line that separates a professional listening experience from a well-intentioned amateur effort.

The Vocal Roll Call

To combat drift, try this practical tactic of the pros. At the start of every session, before you record a single word of new material, spend five minutes reading aloud in the voice of every major character appearing that day. Don't just use your throat—use your body. Posture and physical bearing genuinely affect vocal quality.

The Slouch: If a character is defeated and weary, slouch in your chair while you do their "roll call."

The Spine: If a character is rigid and authoritative, sit bolt upright.

By physically "putting on" the character before you hit record, you remind your muscles and your mind who these people are. It ensures that Brian sounds like Brian, whether it's hour one or hour twenty.

He Said, She Said: The Art of the Invisible Tag

As we've discussed before, in the world of print, the most invisible words in your novel are "he said" and "she said." Throughout this book, I've encouraged you to prune any unnecessary tags to keep the dialogue lean and the pacing snappy. As you review your manuscript for the audiobook, you have the final word on which attributions stay and which go on the cutting room floor.

If the voices and inflections are distinct, you can safely strike many of those tags from your recording script. It pays off in listenability:

Written Page:
"I don't think we should go in there," Charles said.
"Why not? It's just a house," Angela replied.
"It's not just a house, and you know it," he said firmly.

Audio Version:
(In a low tone) "I don't think we should go in there."
(In a defiant, light tone) "Why not? It's just a house."
(Charles again, with weight) "It's not just a house, and you know it."

When the dialogue flows naturally and cinematically, the "he saids" safely disappear into the performance.

Of course, it's not practical to delete every tag. You'll want to keep them in situations such as these:

The "Action" Tag: If the tag includes a vital action (e.g., "he said, slamming the door"), you must keep it or find a way to convey that sound.

The Group Conversation: If there are three or more people in the room, the listener needs those roadmaps to stay oriented. Even a great narrator can only juggle so many distinct voices before they start to run together.

The Rhythmic Beat: Sometimes, a strategically

placed "he said" provides a necessary pause—a moment for the previous line to breathe before the next one hits.

Adding Attributions

There are times when your audiobook might require an attribution that wasn't in your manuscript. Without the visual cue of an indented paragraph to signal a change in speaker, your listener is relying entirely on your vocal shifts. If those shifts are too subtle, the listener can quickly lose their place.

The Ear Test: Before you record, do a specific editorial pass through your dialogue-heavy scenes with one question only: *If I close my eyes and listen to this, will I know who is speaking at every moment?* If the answer is ever "probably not," insert a tag. Your listener's lucidity matters more than a strict adherence to the clean margins of your book.

Avoid Vocal Overlap

In an audiobook, a dialogue tag is the brief moment your listener's ear recalibrates. After a stretch of character-voiced dialogue, the tag is the vital signal that the character has finished speaking and the narrator has resumed control.

In practical terms, this means your delivery of a dialogue tag should be emotionally neutral. If your character is talking in an Australian accent, don't let that affectation bleed into the "he said" that follows. When you hit the tag, snap back to your narrator voice. Blurring the line between character and narrator will confuse the listener who's unsure who's saying what.

The "Said" Beat

Do not rush the tags. Do not swallow them. Give the "he said" a tiny bit of air—a fractional pause before and after. This creates a rhythmic cradle for the dialogue, making the listening experience feel intentional and paced, rather than a breathless race to the finish line.

Knowing Your Limits

By now, I hope you see that I believe in your ability to bring your story to life. It's because of that belief that I want to close this challenging chapter with a brief,

MCCARTHY'S METHOD

Minimalist Cormac McCarthy famously abandoned most "weird little marks" of punctuation, including quotation marks and commas. In masterpieces like *No Country for Old Men*, he relied on a sparse, rhythmic prose style to signify speaker changes, believing that "if you write properly you shouldn't have to punctuate." While this creates a legendary, atmospheric flow on the printed page, it serves as a high-wire act for the narrator. Without the visual road signs of punctuation, his work requires a masterclass in vocal pacing and tone to keep the listener from getting lost in the desert. For the DIY narrator, McCarthy's style is a reminder of the need to strike the right balance between too few and too many dialogue tags.

honest word about limitations. Some characters will genuinely be beyond your range—not because you lack commitment, but because the human voice has physical boundaries. Some accents and vocal characteristics require specialized training to execute convincingly. A character whose entire identity is bound up in a vocal quality you cannot effectively reproduce is a creative problem worth taking seriously.

Remember, you can always *suggest* an accent rather than perform it. What you should *not* do is pretend. A badly executed accent performed with great confidence is the audio equivalent of a typo in the first paragraph—the listener loses confidence in the writer and wonders if the rest of the journey is worth their time.

Knowing your limits is the same editorial judgment you applied to your prose. You've cut the scenes that weren't working; you can make the same clear-eyed decisions about your performance. That isn't giving up. That is professionalism—the most attractive quality a self-narrating author can bring to their audiobook.

The "Technical" Temperament

In order to be a DIY narrator, you will also be handling the "recording engineer" part of the process (unless you happen to be working with a producing partner). This requires a unique temperament: the patience to stay perfectly still, the discipline to monitor your levels in real-time, and the fortitude to stay calm when a neighbor's lawnmower ruins a perfect take.

Likewise, remember that your voice is a muscle that requires stamina. Should you already be leaning into thoughts that the learning curve—or the physical toll—is too steep, that's okay. That is why professionals exist.

But if you're still standing, gear up for some gear talk. In the next chapter, we're going to build your ideal recording studio on a shoestring budget.

CHAPTER 9: THE HOME STUDIO

SETTING UP A SPARE ROOM FOR SOUND

If you've decided to take the DIY plunge, your first instinct is probably to head straight for a tech website and start getting glassy-eyed over $1,000 microphones, professional-grade acoustic foam, and pre-amps with enough glowing lights to land a small aircraft.

Stop. Put the credit card away.

Before you turn your guest bedroom into a NASA control center, remember this: a great audiobook isn't built out of expensive hardware. It's built out of a clean recording and an engaging performance. In 2026, the technology has reached a point where the "entry fee" for a professional-sounding recording studio is lower than it has ever been.

To begin your rough and ready replica of Abbey Road, you really only need two essential tools to bridge the gap between your voice and the listener's ear:

A Reasonably Priced Microphone: You don't need a vintage studio mic that costs as much as a used car. You need a reliable workhorse that captures the natural warmth of your voice without picking up the hum of your refrigerator.

A Digital Audio Workstation (DAW): This is the software where your recording lives. While there are high-end professional suites available, many authors produce award-winning audio using software that is—believe it or not—completely free.

Everything else—the fancy headphones, the adjustable boom arms, the soundproofing panels—is just a supplement to these two essentials. If you have a solid mic and the right software, you have a studio.

The Microphone: Your Sonic Signature

When you start shopping, you'll see dozens of specifications. Most of them are more complicated than we need to concern ourselves with for voice work. The only one you should look for is a "Cardioid" pickup pattern. Think of this as a heart-shaped hearing zone. A cardioid mic listens intently to what is directly in front of it—that is, your mouth—and politely ignores the noise behind it, like the hum of your computer fan or the ghost of a lawnmower three houses down.

The Great Connector: USB vs. XLR

In the world of studio microphones, you'll encounter two ways to plug into your PC:

USB Microphones: These are the "Plug-and-Play" heroes. You plug the mic directly into your computer's USB port, and you're ready to record. No extra boxes, no complicated wiring. For most authors, a high-quality USB mic is the ideal choice.

XLR Microphones: These require an interface (a separate piece of hardware) to bridge the gap between the mic and your PC. While pro studios love them for their versatility, they add a layer of technical complexity (and cost) that many DIYers simply don't need.

The "Short List" for 2026

You don't need to spend a fortune to sound like a million bucks. Here are the current front-runners:

The Budget Workhorse (approx. $100): Look at the Audio-Technica AT2020USB+ or the Rode NT-USB Mini. These are compact, incredibly sturdy, and deliver a clean, crisp sound that punches way above their price tag.

The Versatile Standard (approx. $150): The Blue Yeti (now under Logitech) remains a staple. While it's a bit bulky, it offers a "Gain" knob right on the mic, allowing you to adjust your volume levels without touching your mouse.

The Podcaster's Darling (approx. $400): The Shure SM7B is a legend for a reason—it's the "Michael Jackson mic." (He used it to record *Thriller.*) However, keep in mind it's an XLR mic and requires an interface. If you want that Shure sound with USB simplicity, look at its younger brother, the Shure MV7+. It gives you that rich, "radio-ready" tone with plug and play connectiviity.

You'll be surprised how wildly prices vary between merchants of microphones. Before you click the Buy button, check the major music retailers alongside the big-box sites. Often, you can find a "bundle" that includes a mic stand or pop filter for the same price as the mic alone.

While we're mentioning stands and filters, those are two unsung heroes you'll want to have.

A Mic Stand: Depending on your workspace and mic, choose from a desk stand or a boom arm. A boom clamps to your desk and lets you float the microphone at the perfect height and angle. This keeps the mic away from your keyboard and—more importantly—away from the "thump" of you accidentally bumping the desk.

A Pop Filter: This is that circular mesh screen you see in every studio photo. Its job is to catch plosives—the tiny puffs of air that happen when you say words starting with 'P,' 'B,' or 'T.' Without a filter, that air hits the microphone like a hammer, causing a "pop" that is a pain to fix later. A $15 filter is one of the best insurance policies you'll ever buy.

Choosing Your Engine: The DAW

In order to record, choose a well-known Digital Audio Workstation, or DAW. It's truly a word processor for sound. If you've ever used a tape recorder or captured audio on your phone, you can do this.

While there are dozens of options, most home studio narrators find their home in one of these "Big Four" engines.

1. **Audacity (The Open-Source Hero)**
   - **Cost:** Free
   - **The Vibe:** The "Swiss Army Knife."
   - Best For: Authors on a budget who want a powerful, no-frills tool. It's available for both PC and Mac and has a massive community of users. When you have a question, there are numerous YouTube tutorials waiting for you.

2. **Adobe Audition (The Industry Workhorse)**
   - **Cost:** Monthly subscription
   - **The Vibe:** Industrial Strength.
   - **Best For:** Authors already paying for the Adobe Creative Cloud. Audition offers arguably the best noise-reduction tools in the business.

3. **GarageBand (The Mac Entryway)**
   - **Cost:** Free (Pre-installed on Macs)
   - **The Vibe:** Intuitive and Visual.
   - **Best For:** Mac users who want to start recording immediately. It's essentially a "lite" version of professional music software, making it very easy to navigate for non-techies.

4. **Logic Pro (The "Big Brother")**
   - **Cost:** One-time Purchase
   - **The Vibe:** Professional Grade
   - **Best For:** Those Mac users who have outgrown GarageBand. Logic Pro offers more tools for fine-tuning and better organization for large projects, though it comes with a steeper learning curve.

5. **The Newcomer: Hindenburg Narrator**
   - **Cost:** Subscription or One-Time Purchase
   - **The Vibe:** The "Audiobook Specialist."
   - **Best For:** Authors who want to focus on the story and let the software handle the technicalities. Hindenburg was built specifically for spoken-word narration. It includes a Manuscript Window where you can read your text directly inside the software, and a one-click "ACX Check" that tells you if your audio meets the industry's strict technical standards. It's not free, but the time it saves in technical troubleshooting could be worth the investment.

.

The DIY DAW Goal

You needn't agonize over which software to choose. The physics of sound remain the same. Whether you're clicking a button in Audacity or turning a fader in Audition, the goal is a clean, consistent waveform.

Pick the one that matches your computer and your budget, watch a "Getting Started" video, and spend your energy on the performance. The listener won't know whether you recorded in a $500 program or a free one. Start out easy with a freebie and master that. If you want to move up later, that's always an option.

The "Dry Voice" Requirement

The biggest mistake a DIY narrator makes is thinking that expensive gear can solve a bad room. In the world of audio, the room is your instrument. If you put a world-class microphone in a room with hardwood floors and bare walls, it will simply do a world-class job of recording how much your room echoes. You'll end up with a high-definition recording of a tunnel.

Professional-sounding narration relies on what is known as "dry voice." If you stand in a bathroom and speak, you hear reverb—the sound bouncing off the tiles. In an audiobook, that echo is a dealbreaker. You want your voice to be clean, dry, and "close," with absolutely nothing in the background. (Even if your audiobook will have music and sound effects added, the initial voice track should be pristine.)

To kill the bounce, you need soft, absorbent materials. But you don't need a $2,000 acoustic booth; you just need to get creative. You can create a professional recording environment for less than the cost of a nice dinner out.

The DIY Veteran's "Acoustic Hacks"

The Closet Method: A walk-in closet full of clothes is a natural, reverb-free recording booth. The fabric of your coats soaks up the sound. (Pro tip: Replace regular bulbs with LEDs to avoid turning your booth into a sauna.)

The Mattress Trick: Don't be afraid to lean a spare mattress against a wall near the microphone. It may look ridiculous, but it deadens the room with surprising efficiency.

The Moving Blanket: Heavy, padded moving blankets draped over a PVC frame or even a door can block out unwanted reflections in a noisy house.

The "No-Go" Zones: Avoid kitchens and bathrooms at all costs. The hard surfaces are your enemy, and the hum of a refrigerator or an ill-timed icemaker will ruin a take as quickly as your neighbor's barking dog

Silence Is Louder Than You'd Think

In a typical modern home, silence is rarely silent. Your new, sensitive microphone doesn't just capture every nuance of your fabulous voice; it hears the things your ears have learned to tune out. To the microphone, your peaceful spare room is a minefield of mechanical vibrations.

- **The Computer Fan:** As your processor works to record, it gets hot, and the fan kicks in. Move the computer as far away from the mic as possible—perhaps even under the desk or behind a pillow.

- **Kill the Hidden Noises:** Unplug electronic devices that "hum." Turn off the air conditioner or heater while the mic is live. (Don't worry, you'll remember to turn it back on when the sweat starts to drip!)

- **The Talking Wardrobe:** Avoid "swishy" nylon tracksuits or clicking jewelry. Wear soft clothing. Your microphone is so sensitive it can hear your sleeves rubbing against your sides.

- **Check Your Chair:** A squeaky spring is the bane of a narrator. If your favorite desk chair groans every time you shift your weight, swap it for a solid kitchen chair draped in a blanket.

The Digital Safety Net: Noise Reduction

Some recording software allows you to sample a consistent hum (like a distant fridge) and automatically remove it. This is a powerful tool, but it's not a magic wand. If you overdo the settings, your voice will start to sound underwater or metallic. Aim for a clean recording first; use the software only for the finishing touch.

Almost There

Once your sonic sanctuary is built and your noisy nuisances are neutralized, you are ready to move from Studio Designer to Narrator. But don't hit that red button just yet.

In this next chapter, we're going to map out your game plan. We'll talk about how to avoid errors and how to tackle linguistic goofs without losing your groove. Let's step into the studio and turn those written words into a polished, professional masterpiece.

CHAPTER 10: INTO THE BOOTH
RECORDING WITH A NARRATOR MINDSET

You have set up your studio, silenced the hum in the room, and primed your pipes. Now, you are sitting in front of a computer screen ready to fill it with jagged blue lines—the *waveform*. To a newcomer, this looks like a heart monitor in a high-tech hospital. To a narrator, it's the topographical map of your story.

To keep your focus, you should view audio production as five separate entities. If you try to do all five at once—recording a sentence, then immediately stopping to edit it—you will lose your vocal groove and burn out before you finish the Preface.

The Five Stages of the Audio Assembly Line

Recording: The raw act of speaking. This is where the magic happens.

Editing: The "Cleanup." This is where you remove the clicks, the dog barks, and the three times you tripped over a tongue-twister.

Proofing: The Quality Control. You listen to your audio against the manuscript to ensure you didn't accidentally skip a paragraph or change "house" to "home." (Unless you do indeed want to change it. If it's your book, no law says the audiobook can't be slightly different. More on that in a moment.)

Mastering: The "Polish." This is where we bring the volume and equalization up to industry standards (the "ACX Check").

Uploading: The Finish Line. Sharing your digital files with the world.

Finding the Sweet Spot: Professional Mic Technique

Once your DAW is configured and your levels are set, the most critical hardware in the room is actually you. Professional narration isn't just about the quality of your microphone; it's about your physical relationship to it. New narrators often make the mistake of "eating the mic"—getting as close as possible to achieve a deep, radio-style resonance. If you think about it, no human ear gets that close to your mouth. Putting the mic right at your lips results in "plosives" and an overwhelming amount of mouth noise. To achieve a clean, natural sound that listeners can enjoy for hours, you must find your Sweet Spot.

If you have a pop filter, place it 2 to 4 inches from the mic, and speak into it at about that same distance. In lieu of a filter, a reliable rule of thumb for consistent narration is hand-width distance: Extend your hand, spread your fingers wide, and place your thumb against the microphone and your pinky against your lips. This roughly six-to-eight-inch gap is the professional standard. It provides enough distance for air pressure to dissipate before hitting the capsule—drastically reducing popping—while remaining close enough to capture the warm, intimate nuances of your natural speaking voice.

Beyond distance, *angle* is your secret weapon against sibilance and harshness. Rather than speaking directly into the center of the microphone (on-axis), try the off-axis technique. Rotate the microphone or your body slightly—about 15 to 30 degrees—so that your breath stream passes *across* the face of the mic rather than directly into it.

That simple adjustment will allow the microphone to capture the clarity of your words without the "hurricane" of air that comes with heavy consonants.

Finally, remember that consistency is the key to a seamless edit. If you lean into the mic during an emotional passage and pull back during an action sequence, your volume levels will fluctuate wildly, creating a headache during the mastering phase. Find a comfortable, seated posture that you can maintain for long periods.

Marking Your Script for the Ear

Writing for the eye and reading for the ear are two very distinct disciplines. On the page, a long, elegant sentence is a writer using their creative license; in front of a microphone, it's a lung-busting obstacle ready to trip you up. To ensure a smooth delivery, treat your manuscript like a musical score, and notate away.

The Narrator's Shorthand

Don't rely on your memory or the manuscript's punctuation alone. Use a simple set of visual cues—whether you're using a tablet or a printed page—to tell your brain what's coming next:

The Breath Slash (/): Standard punctuation doesn't always account for your lung capacity. Use a single slash / where you need a breath, even if there isn't a comma. Use a double slash // for a "beat" or a transition where you want the last line to land with the listener.

The Stress Underline: Underline words that carry the meaning of the sentence. Often, we naturally emphasize the wrong word (e.g., "I *don't* have a problem with you" vs. "I don't have a problem with *you*"). Marking these ahead of time prevents robotic reading.

The Character Anchor: Next to a line of dialogue, you may write a single-word cue for the character's "essence." For a gruff character, write "grit"; for a nervous one, write "airy". This anchors your voice before you say the line, ensuring the character sounds the same on page 300 as they did on page 10.

The Warning Circle: Circle words that are tongue-trippers or difficult to pronounce. Seeing a circle five seconds before you hit the word gives you time to prepare for the challenge.

The "Cold Read" Trap

Never record a chapter you haven't read aloud at least once that same day. Your eyes can skim over a typo or a clunky sentence, but your tongue will trip over it. Marking your script is your "dress rehearsal"—it allows you to find the rhythm of the prose so that when the Record light is on, you aren't reading; you're storytelling.

Recording Yourself: Keeping It Real

Before you speak the first word of Chapter One, you have to remember: The microphone doesn't just hear your voice; it hears your intention.

To keep your read consistent, intimate, and professional, follow these pillars of a pro recording session.

1. The "Invisible Audience" (The Photo Trick)

Recording an audiobook can be a lonely business. It is easy to slip into "Announcer Mode"—that stiff, formal voice that sounds like you're reading a traffic report on a CB radio. To combat this, place a small photo of a close friend, a spouse, or even a trusted mentor right behind your microphone.

Why? Because this isn't about narrating to the masses. You are telling a story to one person. When you look at that photo, your tone naturally shifts. Your volume drops, your pacing becomes conversational, and that Walter Cronkite authority becomes an intimate confidence shared between friends. If you feel yourself getting "stiff," look at the photo and remind yourself: "I'm just telling [Name] what happened next."

2. The "Eye-to-Mouth" Delay (Reading Ahead)

A frequent cause of stumbles and tongue-tangles is the line break. Your mouth reaches the end of a physical line on the manuscript, but your brain hasn't processed the first word of the next line yet. Result? A pregnant pause or a tripped-over syllable.

You can overcome this by training your eyes to stay three to five words ahead of your mouth. Think of it like driving a car; you don't look at the pavement directly under your front tires; you look fifty yards down the road. By scanning ahead, your brain can prepare the emotional inflection for the end of the sentence before your vocal cords even get there. This is how you avoid sounding surprised by your own plot twists.

3. The Physical Narrative (Acting It Out)

If you sit perfectly still like a statue to avoid making noise, your voice will sound like that statue. We do want to avoid swishy clothes and squeaky chairs, but we also want the energy of a natural performance.

Don't be afraid to use your hands. If Charles is pointing toward the dark basement, physically point. If Angela is shrugging off a question, physically shrug. These movements change the tension in your chest and the resonance in your throat. Even if the listener can't see you, they can hear the shrug. It adds a layer of unconscious authenticity that makes the characters feel three-dimensional.

4. The Two-Second Tail (aka Seam Allowance)

In the world of sewing, "seam allowance" is the extra fabric left so the pieces can be joined together. In audio, your seam allowance is silence, often called "handles".

When recording, leave two full seconds of silence at the start and end of every paragraph. When you finish a heavy emotional beat, don't rush into the next sentence. Let it breathe. Count to two in your head. In the Digital Workbench phase, these gaps of "room tone" give you the physical space to cut, move, or delete sections without the audio feeling chopped or abrupt.

5. The "Sentence-Back" Rule (The Pick-Up)

When you stumble, the temptation is to just fix the one word you mangled. But that's not a good idea. If you just patch in a single word, it won't be seamless. Your energy, your breath, and your volume will be slightly different than they were three seconds ago.

Same goes for a retake that has a different (perhaps frustrated!) energy than your first take. A sudden increase in volume or intensity screams "edit".

The Fix: Always go back and re-record the entire sentence, perhaps even the previous one as well. By starting the thought from the beginning, you naturally recapture the flow and energy of the original take. When you edit it later, the transition will be invisible.

The $3 Breadcrumb: The Clicker

Our biggest secret to efficient editing isn't expensive software; it's a $3 plastic dog-training clicker.

When you make a mistake—before you go back and reread those words—take your clicker and give it a sharp "CLICK-CLICK." On your screen, this creates a massive, vertical spike in the waveform.

When you go back to edit, you won't have to listen to the whole hour to find the errors. You simply look for the spikes, cut out the dead air and the mistake that happened just before the click, and stitch the clean takes together. It eliminates a needle-in-a-haystack hunt.

The Double-Take Rule for Mispronunciations

Even the most seasoned pros hit a word that they're not sure how to say, even when they've written it! If you stumble upon a word and realize you aren't entirely sure of the pronunciation (is it PRIMM-er or PRIME-er?), you've got two choices:

1. Stop and look it up, which interrupts your flow.

2. Read the sentence both ways and click to mark the spots. You'll have two clean versions with the same vocal attitude to choose from later, rather than a mismatched mess.

Tuning Your Human Hardware

Your voice is a biological instrument. Unlike a guitar, you can't just swap out the strings if they get worn down mid-chapter. To maintain a consistent, professional tone over a four-hour recording session, you need to think about what you're putting into your body.

The Dehydration Trap: Surprisingly, drinking a gallon of water during your session doesn't do all that much to keep your throat lubricated. It takes about 24 hours for water to fully hydrate your vocal tissues. If you're recording on Tuesday, your hydration should start Monday morning.

Temp Matters: Avoid ice-cold water in the booth. Cold water constricts the muscles in your throat. Stick to room temperature or lukewarm water to keep the muscles relaxed. If you prefer hot drinks to wet your whistle, herbal tea is fine, but the caffeine in coffee actually dries the throat.

Booth-Safe Fuel and What to Avoid: Lean protein (ex. turkey, boiled egg) provides sustained energy without the sugar crash of an unhealthy snack. The pectin in green apples reduces mouth noise and clicks.

Avoid dairy (milk, cheese, yogurt) at least four hours before you record. Dairy is a "thickener"—it creates a coating in your throat that will make you sound congested and force you to clear your throat constantly.

The Reflux Warning: Spicy foods, heavy fats, and citrus are the enemies of a long-term narrator. They trigger acid reflux, which burns the edges of your vocal cords, causing hoarseness and a raspy quality that you can't fix in the mix.

The Kindler, Gentler Throat Clear: Repeated loud hacking to clear your throat is like clapping your hands together as hard as you can—it causes physical trauma to the vocal folds. When you feel a tickle or hear unwanted rasp, avoid the violent impact of a cough. Instead, try a gentle, low-pitched growl or a soft hum to vibrate the folds and loosen any vocal congestion.

Follow this with a sip of room-temperature water to sweep your throat clean. This uses your muscles to restore clarity without the wear and tear of a traditional throat clear.This uses the muscles to clear the folds without the violent impact of a cough.

Avoid Menthol: Stay away from mentholated cough drops. They feel refreshing, but they actually dry out your vocal cords, making the problem worse once the initial sensation wears off.

The Hand-Off: From Breath to Bitrate

Now that you've readied your room, mastered mic technique, and validated your voice to carry the narrative weight, you're prepared to breathe life into your book. A YouTube video specific to your DAW of choice will have helped you set up the mic and adjust your recording levels.

Of course, you'll want to some short test runs first to

make sure your voice is recorded and played back with clarity and quality. At that point you can safely go for it and start recording chapters of your book.

The results of your sessions will be a collection of waveforms (in .wav or .mp3 format). On the front end, those digital files of bits and bytes will be like rough-cut diamonds. That is, their brilliance will be hidden beneath layers of stumbles, silences, and the occasional stomach growl.

In the next chapter, we're going to take those raw recordings and tweak them to perfection. I'll show you how to hunt for errors at a glance, how to stitch your best takes into a seamless flow, and how to polish your audio until it's ready for the world's biggest digital stages.

CHAPTER 11: THE ANATOMY OF THE WAVEFORM

EDITING WITHOUT THE MIGRAINE

When you open a digital audio workstation (or "DAW") for the first time—whether it's the free and reliable Audacity, the Mac-friendly GarageBand, or the professional-grade Adobe Audition—it can feel like you've been dropped into the cockpit of a jet fighter. There are knobs, sliders, and glowing green meters everywhere.

Don't panic. You aren't flying a mission to Mars. You only need to know how to navigate the Waveform—the visual heartbeat of your story.

Learning to "See" Your Voice

After recording a section, look at the screen. That jagged line is your voice made visible as a WAV file.

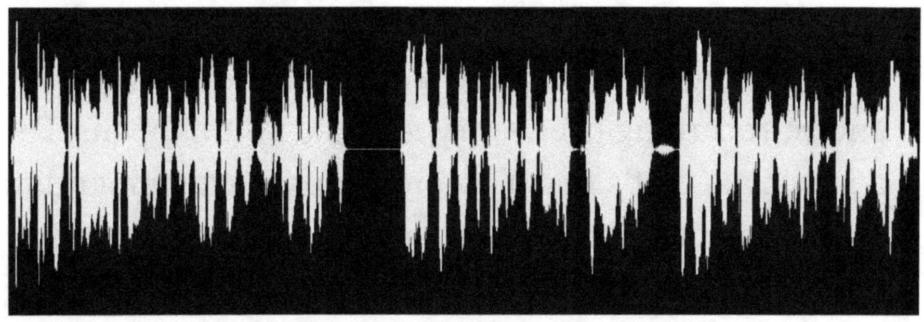

- **The Peaks:** The louder the sound, the taller the "mountain" on the screen.
- **The Valleys:** The flat lines are your silences.
- **The Clicker Spikes:** Remember that dog clicker trick we talked about? This is where it pays off. On your screen, those clicks won't look like speech; they will look like sharp, vertical lightning bolts. Instead of listening back through an hour of audio to find where you coughed, you simply look for the spikes. They say "You Are Here". (Fig. 1)

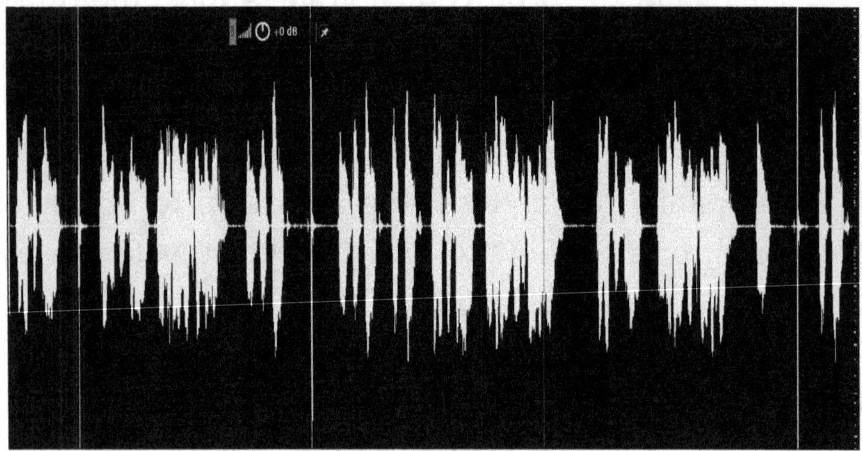

Fig. 1. Waveform showing three clicker spikes

The "Punch vs. Click" Trade-off

Some engineers suggest "Punch and Roll"—stopping and re-recording over every mistake as it happens. For a musician, that's fine. For a narrator, it's a momentum killer. Our dog clicker trick lets you stay in the same vocal performance mode without skipping a beat.

When you go back later to edit your file, zoom in and look for those lightning bolt spikes. Click across the area that includes the spike and the mistake and highlight it (Fig. 2), taking care to replicate the rhythm of the delivery (pauses, etc.). Then join the good takes together by deleting the highlighted area. (Fig. 3)

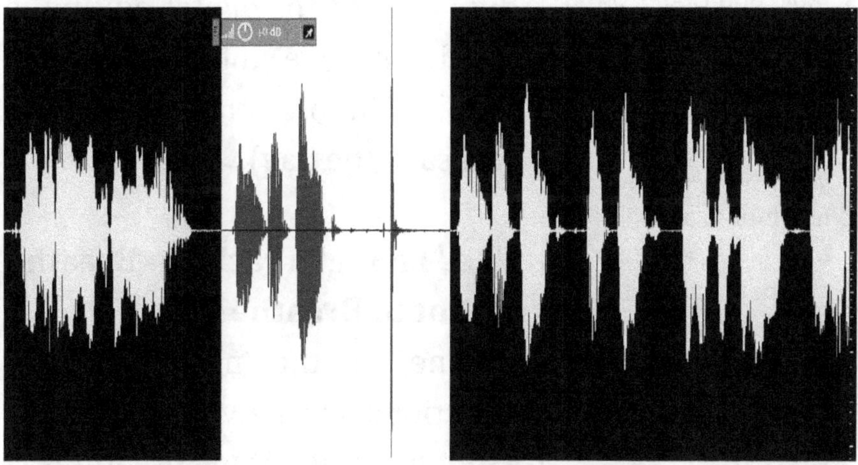

Fig. 2. Before: A highlighted clicker spike and its preceding error

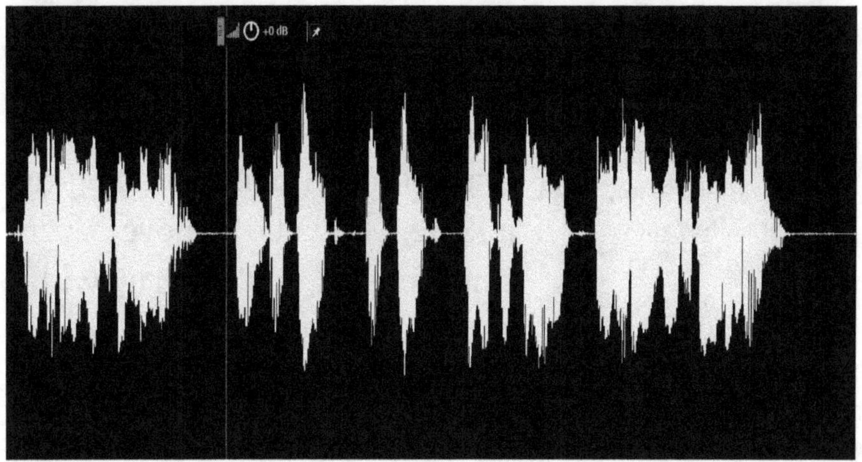

Fig. 3. After: Same waveform after deleting the highlighted range

It's a good practice to leave a tiny bit of blank waveform before and after each edit so you don't accidentally clip the beginning of end of a word. But don't panic if you do delete something you didn't mean to. Digital editing is nondestructive until you save it. Just hit Undo (Ctrl+Z or Cmd+Z will save the day).

THE DIGITAL MIRACLE

Let's take a moment to thank modern technology for something we don't have to do anymore. In the early days of radio and Books on Tape, editing was a literal surgical procedure. If you made a mistake, you would have to find that exact spot on a physical reel of magnetic tape, cut it with a razor blade, and piece the "good" parts together with sticky splicing tape. One sneeze and your chapter was ruined. Today, editing is "non-destructive." If you mess up, you just click "Undo" or move a digital block. It's cleaner, faster, and infinitely more forgiving. Editing projects that used to require four hours of intensive labor now can now be done in 20 or 30 minutes.

The "Living" Track: To Breathe or Not to Breathe?

One of the most frequent questions for new narrators is: "Should I edit out my breaths?"

The simplest answer is a conditional *no.* Breaths are the "white space" of audio. They signal to the listener's brain that a human being is doing the talking. If you remove every single breath, you'll end up with a cyborg narrator that speaks with an unnatural, breathless urgency that actually makes listeners feel anxious.

The Breath Audit

Instead of deleting breaths, you want to manage them. As you scan your waveform, look for these three types:

- **The Emotional Breath:** Keep these. A sharp intake of air before a shocking revelation or a long, weary exhale after a character's defeat is part of the performance.
- **The "Gasp":** If you take a loud, "hitch-like" breath at the start of a paragraph, it can be distracting. Instead of deleting it, use your Gain or Volume tool to turn it down by about 50-70%. This keeps the human rhythm but removes the distraction.
- **The Transparent Narrator:** The objective teller of your tale should remain a voice, not a physical presence. If you breathe too loudly, the narrator accidentally becomes another character in the room. Strive to keep your intakes silent during narration so the focus stays entirely on the prose.

The "Mouth Noise" Minefield

While breaths are human, mouth clicks and saliva pops are just technical noise. Your microphone is so sensitive it will pick up the sound of your mouth opening or the tiny tick of your tongue.

Mouth clicks often look like tiny, sharp specks on your waveform, usually right before or after you speak.

Zoom way in, like we did for the clicks. You can often highlight just that tiny speck and hit Delete.

But what if there's a smack right in the middle of a sentence? Depending on where it falls, you may still be able to excise that tiny fragment without any undue need to undo.

Pacing: The Rhythm of the Story

In a printed book, the reader controls the speed; they can linger on a beautiful sentence or skim through a fast-paced action scene. In an audiobook, you are the pace car.

As you edit your waveform, pay close attention to the silences between your sentences and paragraphs. Each plays a vital role.

The Paragraph Pause: A paragraph break is a visual signal to the reader to take a breath. For most audio, aim for a consistent gap of about 1.5 to 2 seconds between paragraphs.

The "Beat" for Impact: If you've just delivered a shocking plot twist or a profound emotional realization, give the listener an extra second to react to it. Let the moment land.

The Chapter Header: Each individual chapter must be its own audio file. A standard rule of thumb is to have 3 to 5 seconds of silence between chapters, so leave that extra space at the end of each chapter file.

The ACX "Building Codes": Headers and Tails

If you are aiming for Audible (via ACX), they have two non-negotiable rules for the very beginning and very end of your audio files.

The Header: Every file must have 0.5 to 1 second of "Room Tone" before the narration begins.

The Tail: Every file must have 1 to 5 seconds of Room Tone after the narration ends.

If your file cuts off the moment you finish speaking, causing the next chapter to begin a milliseconfd later, it will feel like a jump-scare for the listener. ACX will inevitably bounce your file back for repairs.

So what is Room Tone, you ask? Well, we're getting into the weeds a little bit, but it's something to know.

The Sound of Silence: Understanding Room Tone

When you edit out a mistake, a long pause, or a loud stomach growl, your first instinct might be to simply delete the audio and leave nothing in its place. In the digital world, "nothing" is a flat line—absolute, mathematical silence. Absolute silence is unnatural. To listeners, a sudden drop into total silence sounds like their headphones just died or their internet cut out. It's jarring and unnatural because, in the real world, "quiet" still has a sound.

That is Room Tone (sometimes called "atmosphere" or "air"). It's the subtle, nearly imperceptible hum of your recording space—the sound of the air molecules moving, the faint electrical pulse of your equipment, and the character of your studio.

Even if you use your DAW's noise reduction feature (assuming you don't push it all the way to a zero decibel extreme), there will still be a barely imperceptible amount of Room Tone. You want this. To keep your audiobook sounding consistent, replace any seconds of absolute dead air by copy/pasting the same length of Room Tone. Here's how to record it:

Breathing Room

At the start or end of every recording session, sit perfectly still in your booth for 30 to 60 seconds. Don't move, don't turn pages, and try to breathe as shallowly as possible. This gives you a clean sample of your room's unique signature.

The Patch Technique: When you do an edit that creates absolute silence, copy a small slice of that clean Room Tone and paste it into the gap. This acts as audio glue, seamlessly bridging your takes. By maintaining the presence of the room, the listener never feels like they've been suddenly dropped into a vacuum.

By keeping a consistent bed of Room Tone throughout your file, you ensure that the silence between your words feels like a natural pause rather than a technical glitch.

The "Pickup" Strategy: Patching the Holes

Even with the most careful editing, you will eventually reach the Proofing stage and realize you overlooked something. Perhaps you mispronounced a name, skipped a word, or heard a distant siren that you didn't notice during the heat of the performance.

When you find these gaffes, you have two ways to patch them. Neither is wrong; it simply depends on how your brain—and your schedule—prefers to work.

Method A: The "Stop and Fix"

Some narrators prefer to keep their studio set up and jump back into the booth the moment they find each mistake. This ensures the vibe is fresh in your mind. However, be warned: your voice changes throughout the day. A "patch" recorded at 8:00 AM might sound noticeably different than the narration you recorded at 4:00 PM.

Method B: The Laundry List

A more popular approach is to keep a running list of errors as you find them. Once you've proofed the entire chapter, take that list—your "Pickups"—back into the booth and record them all in one go. It doesn't hurt to record two or more takes with different energy to ensure a match. You then simply copy/paste the better take into your master waveform.

Whether you choose to patch as you go or prefer recording your pickups in a single batch, remember the goal: *invisible* surgery. Your edits should be so seamless that the listener never suspects a digital razor blade ever touched the file. When you can no longer hear where the mistake ended and the correction began, you have mastered the anatomy of your waveform.

But even a perfectly edited file isn't necessarily a finished one. In the next chapter, we'll move into the Proofing phase. Essential for accuaracy, proofing is the disciplined journey where we ensure that the story you wrote is the story you recorded.

Put on your best headphones and find a quiet spot—it's time to hear your book for the very first time.

CHAPTER 12: PROOFING
YOUR ACCURACY INSURANCE

If the recording booth was the stage and the waveform was the workbench, then Proofing is the judge's chambers. This is the point of the process where you transition from Performer and Engineer to Auditor. It is, admittedly, a tedious part of the journey, but it's also where your audiobook earns its professional stripes.

Proofing is the undistracted, highly intentioned act of listening to your edited audio while following along with your manuscript word-for-word. You are looking for two things: Accuracy and Artistry

The Fresh Ears Strategy

First, a rule of thumb: Avoid proofing on the same day that you record. When you've just spent three hours narrating, your brain is echoing. You know what you meant to say, so your mind may hallucinate the correct words even if your mouth stumbled.

To catch your errors, you need fresh ears. Wait a day before you sit down for the big listen. This distance allows you to hear the recording as a listener would, rather than as the person who just performed it.

With manuscript in hand, you are generally striving for 1:1 accuracy. You'd be shocked at how easily the human brain can omit the word "not" or swap "the" for "a," completely changing the tone of a sentence.

However, as I've mentioned previously, you are the author, which gives you the right to revise. If you reach a sentence that looked great on paper but sounds off to the ear, go ahead and change it.

Here's an example of something you might adapt for audio. If your manuscript says, *"I can't believe you did that," he said angrily,* but your performance already sounded angry, feel free to edit out the "he said angrily." Your voice did the work; the words are now redundant.

Or if your script says *He sighed,* you don't need to read the stage direction—just give us the sigh.

Sometimes a sentence is too long to be spoken in one breath. You have the freedom to break it in two for the audio version. Your goal is a listener's edition of your book.

The Time Stamp Pickup List

As you listen back to each chapter (with headphones, preferably), jot down any moments where you spot inaccuracies, a weird noise, or a sentence that needs a retake, noting the time stamp shown on your timeline. While your DAW lets you insert digital "markers," I highly recommend going old-school during proofing via your manuscript and a pen or marker.

Example:

04:12 – Mispronounced "Albuquerque"

08:45 – Nose whistle during the pause

12:10 – Cut the "he shouted" after the shout

By making a note instead of messing with your computer, you stay in Listening Mode rather than Tinkering Mode. Once the chapter is finished, you'll have a concise laundry list of pickups. You can then head back into the booth, record all your fixes in ten minutes, and drop them into the master file.

The Energy Audit

As you listen, keep an eye out for any "vibe shifting". If you recorded the first half of a chapter on a caffeinated Monday morning and the second half on a weary Friday afternoon, the seam might be visible. If the energy drops off a cliff mid-scene, re-record a transition to bridge the gap. You want the listener to feel like the story was shared in one continuous, magical telling.

Avoiding The Song that Never Ends

One of the most subtle—and potentially annoying—habits a narrator can develop is a repetitive vocal cadence. This happens when you start every single sentence with the same upward pitch and end every sentence with the same downward drop.

If your sentences all follow the exact same melodic arc, it becomes a hypnotic, sing-song drone that can make even the most exciting thriller work like a lullaby.

As you proof your work, listen for these repetitive patterns. Use your Pickup List to mark those sections for a redo. Read the passage again, but focus on the unique intent of the sentence. Change your starting pitch. Stretch out a word here, or clip a word there. Your goal is to keep the listener slightly off-balance, eager to hear what comes next, rather than nodding off to a repetitive vocal loop.

The Professional "Out" (Outsourcing)

If the thought of listening to your own voice for twenty hours straight makes you want to hide under the bed, you aren't alone. Many professional authors hire Proofing Services. You send *them* the audio and the PDF; they send you back a time-coded list of every stumble and sneeze. It's an extra expense, but if it saves your sanity and ensures a zero-error product, it's worth it.

The Finishing Touch

Having done all this, take a moment to celebrate. You have a "clean" audiobook. Every word is correct, every breath is intentional, and the story is officially in the can.

But there is one final transformation left. In our final chapter, we're going to take your flaw-free audiobook and give it the professional polishing it deserves.

CHAPTER 13: MASTERING AND UPLOADING

GETTING YOUR AUDIOBOOK READY FOR THE WORLD

You've done the hard work. You've built yourself a studio, performed the story, and done all the fine-tuning to ensure every word is perfect. At this point, your audio is clean and honest—but it might sound a bit plain and unpolished.

Mastering is the final stage where we take that raw, dry voice and give it the professional weight, warmth, and "expensive-sounding" sheen that listeners expect from a major production. Your audiobook will be listened to on a variety of playback devices, and it needs to be optimized to sound its best on any of them.

Easy to Master

If the word "Mastering" sounds intimidating, think of it in terms of a classic 1970s stereo—the kind with the heavy silver faceplate and the glowing amber dials. To get the best sound out of an LP, you didn't just turn it on; you adjust the volume, the bass, and the treble until it feels right for the room.

In the digital world, we are doing the exact same thing, just with different names:

Normalization (Volume): This ensures your book isn't a whisper. It brings the overall level up to a standard height so the listener doesn't have to crank up their earbuds to hear you.

Equalization (Bass & Treble): This is where you adjust the tone. You might add a little warmth to a thin voice or shave off some of the muffled low-end to make your words crisp and clear.

Compression (The Consistency Knob): This is the magic ingredient of professional audio. Compression gently squashes the loudest shouts and lifts the quietest whispers so that your entire performance sits at a comfortable, steady energy level.

Seeing the Difference

Compression isn't merely something you hear; it's something you can see. In this image, you see the raw recording. It looks like a mountain range with jagged, unpredictable peaks and deep, quiet valleys. The audio is clean, but the variations in volume can be jarring.

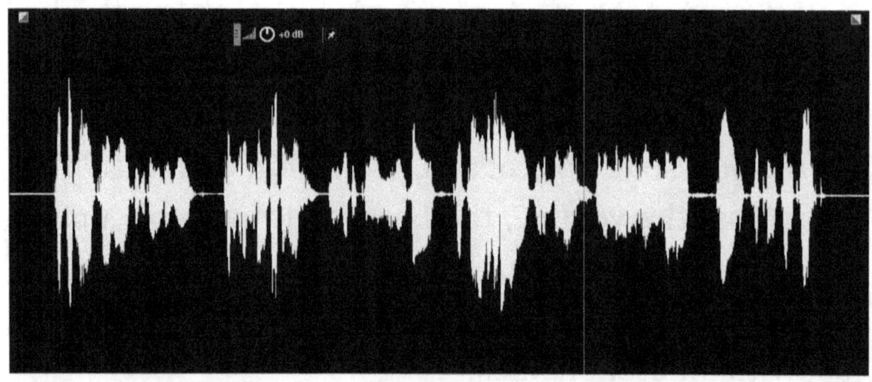

In the image below, you see the same waveform after compression. Now the mountains have been leveled off and the valleys have been filled in. The waveform looks thicker and more consistent. This is the visual signature of a professional audiobook.

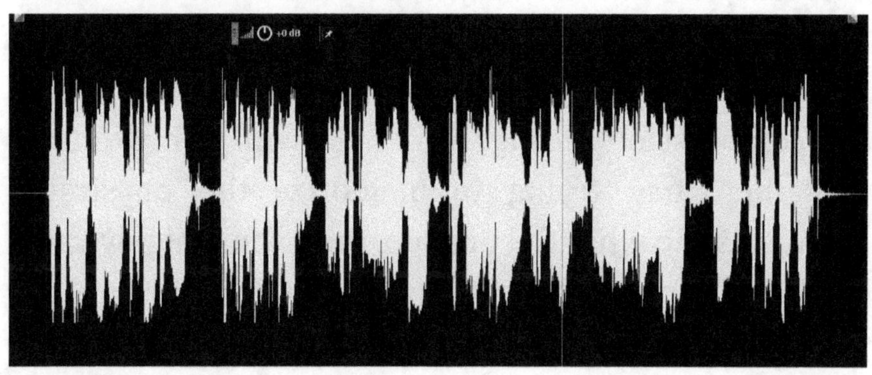

The Car Test

When you're satisfied with the volume, EQ and compression you've applied, export the chapter, put it on your phone, and go for a drive. Don't listen in a quiet driveway; get out on the road. Turn on the heater or the AC. Use your turn signal. If you can still hear the nuances of your performance over the road noise without reaching for the volume knob, you've succeeded. If you sound muffled or like you're speaking through a blanket, go back to your Equalization settings and add a little more highs or upper midrange for clarity.

If you find yourself constantly adjusting the volume during the Car Test, your Compression may not be strong enough. The listener should be able to set the volume once and forget it.

The One-Click Miracle: Macros and Chains

Here is the best news of all: You don't have to be Tesla to handle this tech. And once you've found the ideal settings for mastering your voice tracks, it won't be necessary to manually adjust fifty different dials every time. Most DAWs allow you to use *Macros* or *Chains*. These are essentially presets that apply your volume, EQ, and compression settings all at once with a single click.

Rather than trying to memorize the physics of sound, just do what the pros do: Find some highly-rated YouTube tutorials specifically on "ACX Mastering" for your particular software. Set up your "recipe" once, save it, and then apply it to every chapter. It ensures your first chapter sounds exactly like your last.

The "Specialist" Safety Net

If you reach this stage and all these technical processes make your head spin, remember that you have options. You are a writer. You don't have to be a technician. There are countless specialists who will take your raw, edited files and handle the mastering and ACX technical hurdles for you. If farming out the dirty work allows you to get back to writing your next book, it is money well spent.

CHAPTER 14: LAUNCHING YOUR AUDIOBOOK

THE FINISH LINE AND BEYOND

You've come a long way! After navigating the jet fighter cockpit of your software and polishing your audio until it shines, now comes the most rewarding part: Sharing your voice with the world.

Before you hit that final Submit button on ACX or Findaway, there are a few last-minute hurdles to clear to ensure that your debut sounds—and looks—as professional as a bestseller.

It's Hip to Be Square

In the world of print, your book is a rectangle. In the world of audio, your book is a square. Some authors make the mistake of taking their attractive 6x9 paperback cover and stretching it out to fit the 3000 x 3000 pixel requirement of the audio platforms. It makes the cover look like it's being viewed through a funhouse mirror, and it screams "amateur."

The Fix: If a professional designed your cover, its elements are likely in Photoshop layers. Since they have the original artwork and the titling separated, they can easily rearrange the elements into a square format that feels balanced and intentional.

If you designed the cover yourself, the power is all yours! Take those same layers and resize the imagery. Your title should be bold, readable, and centered. Remember, most people will see this cover on a tiny smartphone screen while they're jogging, so make it pop.

Be sure to add "Read by the Author" (or "Read by [narrator]", if you hired one).

The Gatekeepers: Distribution 101

You don't upload directly to Audible; you go through a distributor. As of this writing, two "Goliaths" dominate: ACX (owned by Amazon) and Findaway Voices (owned by Spotify).

ACX is your direct pipeline to Audible, Amazon, and Apple Books. It's the "Exclusive" path that offers higher royalties but locks you into their ecosystem.

Findaway is the "Wide" path. They'll put your book on Spotify, Google Play, and in thousands of local libraries via apps like Libby.

These free outlets for your audiobook will walk you through the process with their well-designed platforms. Whichever you choose, the process is like the final assembly line. If your files are labeled and mastered correctly, they will click into place like Lego blocks. You are snapping together a single, cohesive unit of your

Opening Credits, the individual chapters, and—very importantly—your Retail Sample.

That five-minute sample is your best salesperson. Don't just start at the beginning of Chapter One. Choose a section of your book that is high-stakes, high-emotion, and leaves the listener dying to know what happens next. You want them to feel like they've just overheard a secret they were privy to know.

The ACX "Red Light": The Automated Judge

When you do upload your files to a distributor like ACX or Findaway Voices, their automated systems will perform a technical scan before a human ever hears a word. If you get a red light for "RMS Levels" or "Peak Floors," don't panic. This is not a critique of your talent; it's a math problem. Most often, it simply means your audio needs a minor volume tweak to play nice with ACX servers. It's a normal part of the professional process. If you hit a wall, refer back to those YouTube tutorials—they often include a specific step for "Peak Limiting" that solves this exact issue in seconds.

Marketing with Your Voice

Once your story is finally live, you might be tempted to simply get on social media and post a linked picture of your cover and a "Please Buy My Book" caption. You can do better than that! In the world of audio, the "Buy" button is rarely pressed by someone who has only seen the book. It is pressed by someone who has heard it. Your voice is your most powerful marketing asset—don't keep it hidden behind a retail wall.

If you have the means, create a short video "trailer" for your audiobook. One of the easiest to make is the Audiogram.

The Audiogram: This is roughly a 30-second video for social media that shows a moving waveform over your square cover while your your most compelling scene plays underneath. Platforms like TikTok, Instagram, and Facebook thrive on this kind of sensory content. If you want people to stop scrolling, give them something to hear.

To create an audiogram, browser-based sites like Headliner, Wavve, or Descript are the standard. These platforms are built specifically for authors and podcasters. You just upload your square cover art, drop in your 30-second audio clip, and choose from a library of "wave patterns" that dance in sync with your voice.

If you are already an Adobe Creative Cloud subscriber, you can achieve the same result using Adobe Express or Premiere. CapCut and Canva are free options you can use to emulate an audiogram, but for most DIY creators, the dedicated audiogram sites offer "one-click" simplicity.

Most of these services offer a "Freemium" model, meaning you can create your first few audiograms for free. However, be aware that free tiers often include a small brand watermark in the corner of your video. If you want a completely clean, professional look for your launch, check the export settings before you finish. Often, a one-month "pro" subscription is worth the small investment just to ensure your book cover—and not the software's logo—is the only thing the viewer sees.

The Review Engine

In the audiobook ecosystem, reviews are the social proof that drive the algorithms. Having said that, an audiobook review should do more than just praise the plot. When you reach out to your early listeners or your street team, encourage them to review the performance. A review that says, "The story was great," is helpful. But a review that says, "The character voices were so distinct that I forgot it was only one person reading," is pure gold. Don't be afraid to ask for that specific feedback; your listeners will often appreciate knowing exactly how they can best support your work.

The Final Word: *You Did It.*

Congratulations! Your silent manuscript is now a living, breathing performance. You have bridged the gap between the page and the soul, and I wish you every success.

Whether you hired a pro to bring your characters to

life or you braved the closet to share your own authentic truth, you have given your story a heartbeat and made it accessible to the commuter, the multitasker, and the visually impaired. Most of all, in a world full of noise, you have contributed something meaningful: a human connection.

Your journey from manuscript to microphone is complete—go forth and be heard.

ABOUT THE AUTHOR

Musician, writer and voice artist Gary Fearon has written over 300 songs, advertising jingles and morning show parodies. He is also a veteran disc jockey and studio producer.

A recipient of the *Billboard* Air Personality of the Year Award, his broadcast work has also been recognized by the Associated Press, *Radio and Production* magazine, and over two dozen MARS awards for commercial production. His voice is heard daily on radio and TV stations across the USA and Canada as well as on audiobooks such as *Eddie: The Life and Times of America's Preeminent Bad Boy*.

Formerly the Creative Director for *Southern Writers* magazine, his published books include *After Abbey Road: The Solo Hits of The Beatles* and *Right Brain Writing: Creative Shortcuts for Wordsmiths.* His short stories appear in multiple compilations including *Stories of Music, Volume II* (Timbre Press, 2017), *Stories from the Attic, Fortune$, Leaves of Wisdom, Memphis Mosaic,* and *At Rest* (AA Inc.)

ALSO BY GARY FEARON

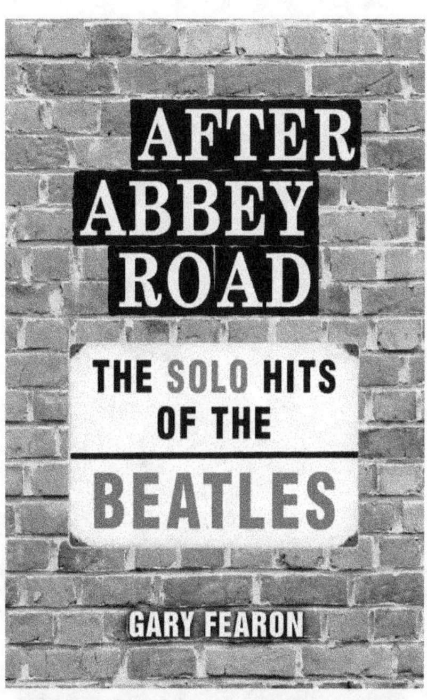

www.ingramcontent.com/pod-product-compliance
Lightning Source LLC
LaVergne TN
LVHW020639100826
845148LV00012B/2244

* 9 7 8 1 7 3 4 8 5 5 5 0 0 *